Your Happy Healthy Pet™

Basset Hound

2nd Edition

GET MORE!
Visit www.wiley.com/
go/bassethound

Terry Albert

Howell
Book House™

Howell Book House
Published by Wiley Publishing, Inc., Hoboken, New Jersey

For general information on our other products and services or to obtain technical support please contact our Customer Care Department within the U.S. at (800) 762-2974, outside the U.S. at (317) 572-3993 or fax (317) 572-4002.

Wiley also publishes its books in a variety of electronic formats. Some content that appears in print may not be available in electronic books. For more information about Wiley products, please visit our web site at www.wiley.com.

Library of Congress Cataloging-in-Publication Data is available from the publisher upon request.

ISBN: 978-0-470-39056-6

Printed in the United States of America

10 9 8 7 6 5 4 3 2 1

2nd Edition

Book design by Melissa Auciello-Brogan
Cover design by Michael J. Freeland
Book production by Wiley Publishing, Inc. Composition Services

About the Author

Terry Albert is a writer and artist specializing in pet-related subjects. She has won several Maxwell Awards from the Dog Writers Association of America for her writing and artwork, and served for several years as their annual writing competition chairperson.

She has had hands-on experience with hundreds of breeds of dogs as a professional dog trainer, at a foster home for numerous breeds, and in more than fifteen years of work as a pet sitter.

Terry has served on the board of directors for Seattle Purebred Dog Rescue and the Humane Society of Seattle/King County, is an active volunteer for several breed rescue groups, and was a founding member of Southern California Labrador Retriever Rescue. She volunteers as a Reserve Park Ranger in the mounted patrol unit in Poway, California. She also received Channel 10 San Diego's Leadership Award for her volunteer work.

Terry's art has been exhibited in the Art Show at the Dog Show and the AKC Museum of the Dog. She also has had numerous commissions from dog breed clubs and private collectors. She currently works from her home, which she shares with her five dogs, two horses, two cats, and two box turtles. She dedicates this book, her first, to the memory of her dad, George Johnson, because he would have been so proud.

About Howell Book House

Since 1961, Howell Book House has been America's premier publisher of pet books. We're dedicated to companion animals and the people who love them, and our books reflect that commitment. Our stable of authors—training experts, veterinarians, breeders, and other authorities—is second to none. And we've won more Maxwell Awards from the Dog Writers Association of America than any other publisher.

As we head toward the half-century mark, we're more committed than ever to providing new and innovative books, along with the classics our readers have grown to love. From bringing home a new puppy to competing in advanced equestrian events, Howell has the titles that keep animal lovers coming back again and again.

Contents

Part I: The World of the Basset Hound   **9**

Chapter 1: What Is a Basset Hound?   **11**
A Scenthound   11
Built for Hunting   12

Chapter 2: Basset Hound History   **17**
French Origins   17
British Influence   18
The Basset Hound in the United States   19
Basset Hounds in Popular Culture   20

Chapter 3: Why Choose a Basset Hound?   **23**
What Bassets Do   23
Natural Instincts   25
Special Needs   26
Temperament and Training   28
Sports for Basset Hounds   30

Chapter 4: Choosing Your Basset Hound   **31**
Decisions to Make   31
Consider a Rescued or Shelter Dog   33
Where to Get a Puppy   35
Questions You'll Be Asked   38

Part II: Caring for Your Basset Hound   **41**

Chapter 5: Bringing Your Basset Hound Home   **42**
Using a Crate   42
Puppy Essentials   43
Puppy-Proofing Your Home   46
Toys   48
Identification   48
Choosing a Name   49
Bringing Your Puppy Home   50
The First Few Weeks   51
Children and Your Puppy   52
Beginning Training and Socialization   54

Chapter 6: Feeding Your Basset Hound   **57**
Feeding Puppies   57
Feeding Adult Dogs   58
Feeding Senior Dogs   60
What to Feed Your Basset Hound   60
Reading Dog Food Labels   64
The Overweight Basset Hound   64
Picky Eaters   66
Poisonous Foods   67

Chapter 7: Grooming Your Basset Hound   68
Grooming Supplies   68
Bath Time   69
Nail Trimming   73
Ear Cleaning   74
Teeth Cleaning   74
Skin Check   75
Making Your Environment Flea Free   76

Chapter 8: Keeping Your Basset Hound Healthy   78
Choosing a Veterinarian   78
Health Concerns for Basset Hounds   79
Common Canine Health Problems   86
Parasites   90
How to Make a Canine First-Aid Kit   93
First Aid   95
When to Call the Veterinarian   98
The Senior Citizen   99

Part III: Enjoying Your Basset Hound   103

Chapter 9: Training Your Basset Hound   104
Understanding Builds the Bond   105
Practical Commands for Family Pets   111
Training for Attention   120
Teaching Cooperation   122

Chapter 10: Housetraining Your Basset Hound   123
Your Housetraining Shopping List   124
The First Day   125
Confine Your Pup   127
Watch Your Pup   131
Accidents Happen   132
Scheduling Basics   133

Appendix: Learning More About Your Basset Hound   136
Books   136
Magazines   138
Clubs, Registries, and Associations   138
Internet Resources   139

Index   141

Shopping List

You'll need to do a bit of stocking up before you bring your new dog or puppy home. Below is a basic list of some must-have supplies. For more detailed information on the selection of each item below, consult chapter 5. For specific guidance on what grooming tools you'll need, review chapter 7.

☐ Stainless steel food dish   ☐ Dog toothbrush and toothpaste

☐ Stainless steel water dish   ☐ Ear cleaner

☐ Dog food   ☐ Chew toys

☐ Leash   ☐ Toys

☐ Collar   ☐ ID tag

☐ Crate   ☐ Pet gate

☐ Nail clippers   ☐ Enzymatic odor remover

☐ Grooming tools (shedding blade, grooming glove, curry comb)

There are likely to be a few other items that you're dying to pick up before bringing your dog home. Use the following blanks to note any additional items you'll be shopping for.

☐ _____

☐ _____

☐ _____

☐ _____

☐ _____

☐ _____

☐ _____

☐ _____

☐ _____

☐ _____

Pet Sitter's Guide

We can be reached at (___)_____-_____ Cell phone (___)_____-_____

We will return on _____ (date) at _____ (approximate time)

Dog's Name _____

Breed, Age, and Sex _____

Spayed or Neutered? _____

Important Names and Numbers

Vet's Name _____ Phone (___)_____- _____

Address _____

Emergency Vet's Name _____ Phone (___)_____- _____

Address _____

Poison Control _____ (or call vet first)

Other individual (someone the dog knows well and will respond to) to contact in case of emergency or in case the dog is being protective and will not allow the pet sitter in. _____

_____

Care Instructions

In the following blanks, let the pet sitter know what to feed, how much, and when; when the dog should go out; when to give treats; and when to exercise the dog.

Morning _____

Afternoon _____

Evening _____

Medications needed (dosage and schedule) _____

Any special medical conditions _____

Grooming instructions _____

My dog's favorite playtime activities, quirks, and other tips _____

_____

_____

(Person's name) _____ has my permission to provide veterinary care for my dog (dog's name) _____in an emergency. I will accept financial responsibility for the dog's care.

Signed _____ Date _____

Owner's name (printed) _____

Part I

The World of the Basset Hound

The Basset Hound

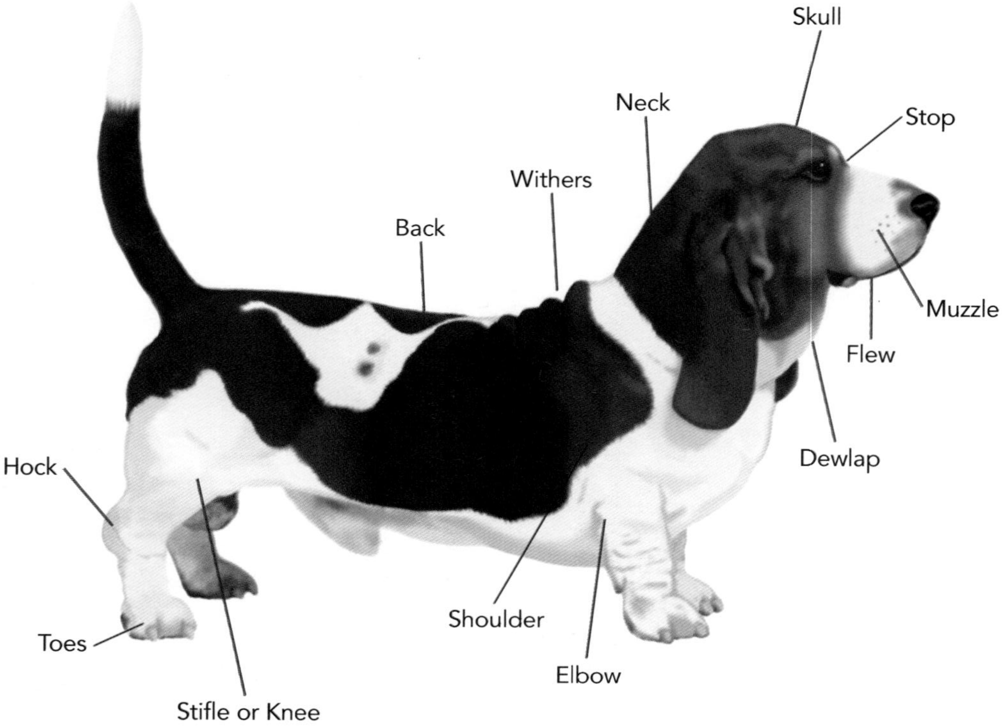

Skull

Stop

Muzzle

Flew

Dewlap

Neck

Withers

Back

Shoulder

Elbow

Stifle or Knee

Hock

Toes

Chapter 1

What Is a Basset Hound?

The Basset Hound's looks belie his personality at almost every turn. Often called "the clown of the dog world," the Basset's greatest joy comes in making family and friends laugh—unless, of course, he's engaged in another favorite activity, like snoozing on the couch or following his nose in pursuit of a rabbit.

As with most breeds, the Basset Hound's form relates directly to its function, although that form will differ to some extent from one dog to another. However, certain physical characteristics combine to define a dog as a Basset Hound. He was bred to follow the scent of a rabbit or hare along the ground, to pursue his quarry single-mindedly. For this purpose, early Basset breeders chose breeding stock that fit their blueprint for both a dedicated and focused personality and a strong, low-slung physique.

The Basset Hound's good temperament has made it a popular breed today, when a dog is much more likely to be a pet than a hunter. You can count on a Basset Hound to be both a strong scenthound and a loving companion.

A Scenthound

When you look at the dogs in the American Kennel Club's Hound Group, you will find scenthounds (dogs who use their outstanding sense of smell to follow game), including Basset Hounds and Beagles, and sighthounds (dogs who hunt by sight as they run down their quarry at great speed), such as Borzoi and Greyhounds. The Basset nose is among the keenest of all breeds—second only to his cousin, the Bloodhound—enabling him to easily follow his quarry.

First and foremost, a Basset Hound is a scenthound who hunts with his nose.

A hunting pack of Bassets finds a rabbit's scent and follows the line (trail) of the scent on the ground. The fleeing rabbit will often change directions suddenly, causing the dogs to sometimes lose the line and have to search until they pick up the scent again. The hunters follow on foot, which is why the Basset's slow pace is an advantage.

The short legs are no deterrent to the Basset Hound's agility. Despite their low stature, these hounds are capable of following a scent over all terrain, through thick brush and shallow streams (although they are not too fond of water). Following the scent is everything to a Basset, and he will go for miles, never giving up on his quest to find the rabbit at the end of his hunt.

Built for Hunting

The Basset Hound breed standard originally used in the United States was written by Sir Everett Millais of Britain in the late 1800s, and was followed until the Basset Hound Club of America approved its own breed standard in 1955. Revised in 1964, it has served since then as the blueprint for the Basset Hound's appearance. The box on page 13 explains what a breed standard is.

Why does the breed standard matter to you? Your hound's personality and physical characteristics are directly related to his role as a hunter. You will better understand what to expect from him, even though he may never hunt for more than a biscuit under the bed. The breed standard is what makes a Basset a Basset.

What Is a Breed Standard?

A breed standard is a detailed description of the perfect dog of that breed. Breeders use the standard as a guide in their breeding programs, and judges use it to evaluate the dogs in conformation shows. The standard is written by the national breed club, using guidelines established by the registry that recognizes the breed (such as the AKC or UKC).

Usually, the first section of the breed standard gives a brief overview of the breed's history. Then it describes the dog's general appearance and size as an adult. Next is a detailed description of the head and neck, then the back and body, and the front and rear legs. The standard then describes the ideal coat and how the dog should be presented in the show ring. It also lists all acceptable colors, patterns, and markings. Then there's a section on how the dog moves, called *gait*. Finally, there's a general description of the dog's temperament.

Each section also lists characteristics that are considered to be faults or disqualifications in the conformation ring. Superficial faults in appearance are often what distinguish a pet-quality dog from a show- or competition-quality dog. However, some faults affect the way a dog moves or his overall health. And faults in temperament are serious business.

You can read all the AKC breed standards at www.akc.org.

Size and Weight

The Basset Hound was developed to perform a specific task with optimum efficiency, and his appearance relates directly to this assignment. He was developed to be a trailing hound who could find and follow the scent of a rabbit on the ground through dense brush over great distances. This required a somewhat low dog, so the Basset should be twelve to fourteen inches tall at the withers (the top of the shoulders). Taller than fifteen inches is a severe fault in this breed.

Although short, he is by no means a small dog. Bassets weigh anywhere from fifty to seventy-five pounds at maturity. In reality, a Basset Hound is a large dog on

The Basset is a dwarf breed. He carries two-thirds of his weight in the front, and his forearms curve under him to support his heavy body.

short legs, and the standard reflects this, describing "a short-legged dog, heavier in bone, size considered, than any other breed of dog." (*Heavy in bone* means substantial—large bones on short legs.)

Body

The Basset Hound is a dwarf, a manmade breed, and his large body may look awkward compared to other breeds. Robert E. Booth, a prominent Basset Hound breeder and judge, wrote in *The Official Book of the Basset Hound* that a true dwarf is characterized as "smaller in size, in which the cartilage of the bone ends grows improperly. The results are stunted limbs, curved bones, large joints, stubby paws, and large heads. . . . [B]ecause of man's intervention we have many dwarfed breeds, of which the Basset Hound is one."

The Basset carries two-thirds of his weight on his front end. The forearms are crooked, and the front legs are under him to support the deep, full chest. His heavy paws have tough, thick pads to protect him as he moves through thorny brush. A long, full rib cage supports his long, low back, and strong hindquarters propel his heavy body through the field.

The Basset Hound's tail usually has a white tip and is carried up and gaily like a flag, in typical hound fashion, so the hunter can see it and follow him through the underbrush.

Head

A Basset Hound's head is an elegant piece of art. Here again, form follows function. When his head is lowered, those marvelous wrinkles and low-set, long ears stir up the scent on the ground and bring it up to his nose. Under his neck there is a pronounced dewlap (folds of skin) that also helps him gather in the scent of his prey.

The standard calls for soft, sad, dark eyes, and that is part of what makes a Basset's expression so endearing. A prominent haw, the sagging lower eyelid, is normal.

Coat and Colors

The standard states "the coat is hard, smooth, and short, with sufficient density to be of use in all weather." The wash-and-wear coat does shed, however. It is also somewhat oily, to repel dirt and water. This sometimes causes a hound odor, or doggie smell, that is more prominent in Bassets than in other breeds.

The Basset Hound can be any recognized hound color. What does that mean? It doesn't matter what the markings are, as long as he is some combination of black, white, and brown, with the brown ranging from rich mahogany red to a pale lemon. Tricolor is most common, followed by red and white (with no black in the coat).

A Basset's head is designed to channel scent to his formidable nose. The sagging lower eyelid is normal.

Tricolor Bassets can be brown with a black saddle marking, like a Bloodhound, or the pattern can be open, meaning random patches of brown and black on a white dog, or random patches of white on a brown and black dog. He can have ticking (freckles) anywhere on the body and legs. A red dog can be red with almost no white, or white with red patches.

So-called lemon coats are very rare, and these puppies are born pure white with a pale tan color appearing at a few weeks of age. A Basset's pattern will continue to change slightly until he is an adult, so don't buy a puppy solely because you love his markings.

Beware of breeders who offer a "rare" blue Basset Hound. The blue (actually gray) is a recessive genetic trait, and some inherited health problems are associated with it, such as allergies. A blue puppy might occasionally be born, but anyone who breeds specifically for the blue color is not a responsible breeder.

A Surprising Athlete

The breed standard tells us the often-forgotten truth about the breed: "It is capable of great endurance in the field." A good hunter needs physical stamina, so a Basset will be very active when young, and capable of long walks and energetic play as he matures. The couch potato image makes for great family photos, but the real Basset Hound emerges after his nap, ready to play and follow his nose wherever it takes him, however long it takes him to get there.

The Basset was bred to be a hunting dog and is a surprisingly able athlete.

Temperament

His determination is equal or superior to his athletic ability. The Basset's role as a scenthound is responsible for many of the breed's personality characteristics, including independence. There is little we humans can do to assist the Basset Hound (or any scenthound) in carrying out his mission to hunt using his keen sense of smell.

This same characteristic makes him a challenge to train, since pleasing you is not his number-one motivation. Basset Hounds are known to be loyal and devoted to their owners, and this devotion, along with a few treats, will help you overcome his less endearing stubbornness.

Bassets are meant to hunt in a pack. Therefore, their good nature extends to friendship with other canines.

Although the official breed standard doesn't address the Basset Hound's distinctive voice, it is expected that while on the trail of game, the hound will "give tongue"—in other words, howl—so the hunter knows he is following the quarry. In your home, that same deep voice announces the arrival of visitors or demands that you open the back door to let him in.

No matter what he looks like, your Basset Hound will be noble in carriage, kind in demeanor, and distinguished in his every aspect. Except maybe when he's wearing his bunny suit.

Chapter 2

Basset Hound History

The beloved hound flopped on your living room floor is a contemporary breed with an ancient heritage. Figures of a dog with the same proportions as the Basset Hound have been found on an Egyptian monument erected before 2000 B.C.E. Early Assyrian dog sculptures also display Basset Hound–like features. Although ancestors of the Basset may have existed in one form or another in these ancient civilizations, it was the French and the British who developed this breed into the scenthound we know today.

French Origins

There is more than one theory about the origin of the Basset Hound in France. Traditionally, the French called all breeds shorter than sixteen inches at the withers *Basset*. The word *bas* means "low-set" in French, and the word *basset* was included in the name of a variety of breeds—though experts do not agree on how many of these *basset* breeds contributed to today's Basset Hound.

The theory most widely accepted is that the breed descended from the St. Hubert's Hound. Developed around the year 700 by the monks in the Abbey of St. Hubert in France, the St. Hubert's Hound was considered the forerunner of all modern scenthounds. They were strong, short-legged hounds that were described as very good at following scent.

However, some Basset Hound historians believe the true ancestors are the Basset Normand and the Basset d'Artois. These were smaller versions of a large French hunting hound, and were developed during the sixteenth century in the Normandy and Artois regions of France. By the nineteenth century, the Comte

A Basset Hound Relative

The Petit Basset Griffon Vendéen (PBGV) is a distant cousin to the Basset Hound, but is not a variety of the same breed. The PBGV (which originated in the Vendée region of France) is a wire-coated (griffon), smaller, almost terrier-like hound with longer legs and a shorter body than the Basset Hound.

Don't think of the PBGV as a wire-coated Basset Hound. Although the PBGV's function is similar to the Basset's, its temperament is not. This is an extremely active and playful breed. If you want a more relaxed, laid-back dog, you should stick with the Basset Hound. Though PBGVs certainly have their charm, only those who enjoy perpetual motion should own one.

Le Couteulx and Monsieur Lane used the Basset Artois and Basset Normand in their kennels to develop the forerunners of the modern Basset Hound. The Basset Hound was developed for a specific purpose. The French hoped this dwarf breed would be able to trail animals at a slower pace than other hounds, thus making it possible for hunters to follow their dogs without riding on horseback. The dog's short legs would also enable the Basset Hound to keep her nose close to the ground through heavy brush without tiring.

This new hunting hound was a great success. Originally used for trailing deer and boar, the Basset soon became a favorite for hunting smaller game, such as hare, pheasant, and rabbit.

British Influence

Although there is evidence of the short-legged hounds in France probably as early as the 1500s, the first of these dogs didn't find their way to Britain until the mid-1800s. From this French breeding stock, the British developed a heavier-boned dog with a Bloodhound-type head.

In 1894, British breeder Sir Everett Millais, apparently dissatisfied with the effects of inbreeding on his Basset Hounds, used artificial insemination to crossbreed a Basset Hound dog to a Bloodhound bitch. The Basset Hound anatomy prevailed through the crossbreeding, and although that first litter was uniformly Bloodhound color (black and tan), follow-up breedings with these puppies produced tricolors and gave Sir Everett what he was looking for: larger, healthier hounds. Early British breeders also bred some Basset Hounds to Beagles, striving to further improve the dogs' hunting ability.

Hunting with Basset Hound packs gained popularity in Britain, and later extended to the United States, where game was hunted in its natural habitat with a pack of at least ten hounds.

The Basset Hound we know today was developed in Britain as a short-legged hunting dog with a head somewhat like a Bloodhound.

The Basset Hound in the United States

The first information about the Basset Hound coming to America appears in George Washington's diaries. His friend, French general the Marquis de Lafayette, sent several to Washington after the Revolutionary War.

Lord Aylesford brought a brace (pair of hounds) to his Big Springs, Texas, ranch for rabbit hunting in 1883—the same year a British show dog, Nemours, was sent to New Jersey. Nemours made his show ring debut in the United States in the spring of 1884 at the Westminster Kennel Club Dog Show, introducing the breed to the American public.

The first Basset Hounds registered with the American Kennel Club (AKC) were Bouncer and Countess, in 1885. In 1935, the Basset Hound Club of America was formed, and in 1937 it became an official member of the American Kennel Club. In that same year, the club held the first Basset Hound field trial, which tests the Basset's ability to find and follow the scent of a rabbit. Many of the dogs of this era competed both in the field and in the show ring. They were truly versatile, dual-purpose dogs.

Throughout the breed's history, Bassets have proved to be versatile dogs, doing well both in the show ring and in the field.

Crossbreeding continued in the United States. In the early 1900s, brothers Carl and George Smith are said to have imported Russian Basset Hounds of French and German origin to be bred to Beagles. They later bred their hounds to French and British Bassets. Robert E. Booth writes in *The Official Book of the Basset Hound*, "In today's Basset Hound history there are twentieth-century Beagles, Bloodhounds, and, most likely, some rather large nineteenth-century Dachshund-type (Basset Allemande) blood too!"

Famous Basset Hound Owners

Harry Anderson

Richard Dean Anderson

Clint Eastwood

Peter Falk

Rex Harrison

Bob Hope

James Earl Jones

Arthur Miller and Marilyn Monroe

George Washington

Anson Williams

Basset Hounds in Popular Culture

In William Shakespeare's *A Midsummer Night's Dream*, Theseus describes his hunting hounds—probably Basset Hounds—this way:

What Is the AKC?

The American Kennel Club (AKC) is the oldest and largest pure-bred dog registry in the United States. Its main function is to record the pedigrees of dogs of the breeds it recognizes. While AKC registration papers are a guarantee that a dog is pure-bred, they are absolutely not a guarantee of the quality of the dog—as the AKC itself will tell you.

The AKC makes the rules for all the canine sporting events it sanctions and approves judges for those events. It is also involved in various public education programs and legislative efforts regarding dog ownership. The AKC has also helped establish a foundation to study canine health issues and a program to register microchip numbers for companion animal owners. The AKC has no individual members—its members are national and local breed clubs and clubs dedicated to various competitive sports.

My hounds are bred out of the Spartan kind,
So flew'd, so sanded, and their heads are hung
With ears that sweep away the morning dew;
Crook-kneed, and dew-lapp'd like Thessalian hulls;
Slow in pursuit, but match'd in mouth like bells. . . .

Basset Hounds appear in French paintings dating to the mid-1800s. Between 1890 and 1910, British painter Arthur Wardle painted Bassets belonging to Queen Victoria and her son, Edward VII. There are also numerous fine sculptures of Basset Hounds, including one that is on display in the library of the AKC, donated by the Basset Hound Club of America.

In contemporary culture, the breed has earned a reputation for humor. The Basset Hound will be forever linked to Elvis Presley, who sang "You Ain't Nothin' but a Hound Dog" to a Basset Hound named Sherlock on *The Steve Allen Show* in the mid-1950s. The Basset's popularity soared in the 1960s when the television series *The People's Choice,* starring Jackie Cooper and Cleo the

The Basset Hound is an iconic image in our popular culture.

Basset Hound, captivated viewers. Around the same time, the Basset Hound became the logo for Hush Puppies shoes.

More recently, the dog Quincy made an occasional appearance on the series *Coach*. Other celebrity Basset Hounds include Flash, a regular on the television series *The Dukes of Hazzard*, Socrates in *Judging Amy*, and Sam on *That's So Raven*. A Basset Hound also keeps company with the lonely Maytag appliance repairman.

In movies, Basset Hounds have appeared in *Spider-Man 2, Smokey and the Bandit*, and *The Rage: Carrie 2*. My personal favorite is Lafayette, the animated Basset who appeared in the 1970 film *The Aristocats*, from Walt Disney Pictures.

Many fans were drawn to the breed through the comic-page antics of *Fred Basset*, whose creator, Scottish cartoonist Alex Graham, clearly had a wealth of experience with this lovable clown of the dog world. Graham based the strip on his own Basset Hound, Frieda.

The frequent appearance of these spokes-Bassets has made the breed increasingly popular. After all, who could resist such a face?

Chapter 3

Why Choose a Basset Hound?

I t seems the Basset Hound was custom made for a family with a sense of humor. Whether snoring in the corner or wearing bunny ears, he'll take over your heart and home as soon as he moves in. But is a Basset Hound the right breed for you?

What Bassets Do

Friendly, easygoing, and affectionate, the Basset Hound is a loyal and loving family member. There's a reason you see so many photos of Bassets playing dress-up with the kids: They love it! Your hound will also love going on outings with you, riding in the car, and joining you for picnics and family gatherings. The Basset Hound is a real family dog. Not attached to just one person, he adores everyone equally.

Bassets love children, provided both children and dog are supervised and taught to treat each other with respect. A rambunctious Basset can knock over a child (or even an adult), and needs to learn from puppyhood not to jump or play too rough.

Your Basset won't be a much of a guard dog, since he loves to meet new people. The good news is that he won't be overprotective of your household either—a benefit if you have lots of visitors and children coming and going. You'll make friends everywhere you go with a Basset Hound. Your pet will be a great ambassador for the breed because people, especially children, will love meeting him. There is a huge social network of Basset owners in many communities who have regular picnics and other get-togethers.

Consider your lifestyle before you get a Basset Hound. Although the Basset needs exercise, this is not a high-energy breed. He's not the dog to play Frisbee or go jogging with you.

You will read over and over that a Basset Hound is a laidback couch potato, a low-energy dog. But a lazy hound will quickly become a fat, unhealthy hound if he doesn't get any exercise. This hunting dog was bred to work for hours at a slow, even pace, so he'll make the perfect walking companion. In fact, he'll *need* to be walked regularly.

All puppies are cute, especially Bassets, but they grow up quickly and become big, heavy dogs. Are you fond of large dogs? The average person will have a hard time lifting one.

Because of his size and low, heavy structure, a Basset Hound cannot swim well. Trotting through a shallow creek is one thing, but a swimming pool presents a real danger. If you have a pool, you will need to fence it to protect your dog, or provide a separate, safe area for him when he is outside.

Basset Hounds grow up to be pretty big dogs. They'll need exercise, too—but not high-energy exercise.

Do you live in an apartment? Basset Hounds make great apartment dogs, with a few exceptions. If you live on an upper floor and there's no elevator, stairs are a problem. The Basset is built with two-thirds of his weight on the front end, and going down stairs could send him head over heels if he moves too fast. Puppies and older dogs can't really handle stairs at all, and an adult dog is too heavy to carry up and down.

Basset Hounds drool. Their droopy lips efficiently collect scent while they hunt. But at home, those same lips collect water and saliva. A good shake of the head will leave dog drool hanging from your ceiling fan and dripping down the wall. Many owners keep a slobber rag by the water bowl.

Natural Instincts

The Basset Hound is first and foremost a scenthound. What does this mean to you? Your Basset is hardwired to follow a scent wherever it leads him. You'll need a yard with a sturdy fence, and you can never let him off leash in an unfenced area because he *will* leave and he won't necessarily be able to find his way home. Bassets were developed to hunt for hours through brush-covered terrain, and he can go for miles before he gives up on an enticing smell. He might end up in an animal shelter in another city, and unless he has identification, you will never get him back.

Bassets follow their nose wherever it leads, and that could lead your dog away from you.

Characteristics of the Basset Hound

Independent

Sensitive

Friendly

Outgoing

Loves children

Loyal

Stubborn

Clownish

The Basset Hound typically shows no fear of traffic and no common sense in dealing with it. Bassets have been known to take a nap in the middle of a road if they tire of the chase and decide to take a break.

It takes only a split second, and an amazingly small opening, for a Basset Hound to scoot out an open door or under a fence and be gone. Children and visitors to the household should be watched carefully to make sure doors and gates are not left open or held ajar while a departing guest stops to engage in one last bit of conversation.

A pet Basset Hound was not meant to live alone. Bassets were used for hunting in packs of two to ten hounds or even more, living and working together. You are your dog's pack. He needs to be indoors with you when you are home, and he will do best with another dog in the household, although it doesn't have to be another Basset Hound. If you are away at work all day, a canine companion is even more important.

A Basset hunting in the field howls as he trails his quarry. This trait is less charming in your backyard. A lonely Basset may howl endlessly, dig, and maybe even tear up the yard or house.

Special Needs

Although the Basset Hound's smooth coat makes him a wash-and-wear breed, he does have grooming needs that cannot be neglected. Are you willing to clean his ears regularly to prevent infection? The Basset's naturally oily coat holds odors and dirt more than other breeds. The wrinkles retain moisture, which can cause skin problems. This is a breed that sheds a lot; can you commit to weekly brushing? If you don't keep up with minimal grooming chores, your Basset will smell bad and shed hair all over the house. If you are obsessive about keeping your house clean, are you still willing to deal with a Basset Hound?

If you are going to let your dog up on the couch, a washable blanket should be placed on his sleeping spot and cleaned weekly. Keep his bedding fresh by adding odor neutralizer to the wash load. Leather furniture is easier to keep clean, and the doggy smell won't weave its way down into the leather.

The Dog's Senses

The dog's eyes are designed so that he can see well in relative darkness, has excellent peripheral vision, and is very good at tracking moving objects—all skills that are important to a carnivore. Dogs also have good depth perception. Those advantages come at a price, though: Dogs are nearsighted and are slow to change the focus of their vision. It's a myth that dogs are color-blind. However, while they can see some (but not all) colors, their eyes were designed to most clearly perceive subtle shades of gray—an advantage when they are hunting in low light.

Dogs have about six times fewer taste buds on their tongue than humans do. They can taste sweet, sour, bitter, and salty flavors, but with so few taste buds it's likely that their sense of taste is not very refined.

A dog's ears can swivel independently, like radar dishes, to pick up sounds and pinpoint their location. Dogs can locate a sound in 6/100 of a second and hear sound four times farther away than we can (which is why there is no reason to yell at your dog). They can also hear sounds at far higher pitches than we can.

In their first few days of life, puppies primarily use their sense of touch to navigate their world. Whiskers on the face, above the eyes, and below the jaws are sensitive enough to detect changes in airflow. Dogs also have touch-sensitive nerve endings all over their bodies, including on their paws.

Smell may be a dog's most remarkable sense. Dogs have about 220 million scent receptors in their nose, compared to about 5 million in humans, and a large part of the canine brain is devoted to interpreting scent. Not only can dogs smell scents that are very faint, but they can also accurately distinguish between those scents. In other words, when you smell a pot of spaghetti sauce cooking, your dog probably smells tomatoes and onions and garlic and oregano and whatever else is in the pot.

Bassets have a scent that is all their own. Don't be fooled by that short coat; it needs a lot of care.

Because of his size and build, a Basset needs help getting in and out of the car or up onto a couch or bed. You may need to provide a ramp or stairs. Up until at least 1 year old, a Basset Hound pup should not be allowed to jump at all. His bones are still growing and joints forming. Teach your dog to wait for you to help him up and down. Even as an adult, he can injure himself if he lands incorrectly.

Temperament and Training

Big, sad puppy-dog eyes can wheedle a lot of table scraps out of a sympathetic owner. And a Basset Hound will work it for all he can get. This really is an intelligent and sometimes manipulative breed, and his reputation for stubbornness is unmatched.

Hound breeds are not Labrador Retrievers, who fetch a bird on command, or Border Collies, developed to help a shepherd with his flock. A Basset was bred to hunt independently, with endless patience and endurance. A Basset Hound owner needs to be equally patient and determined. Your hound wants to know what's in it for him and will try to convert you to his way of thinking. Stubborn, yes; stupid, never!

Most Basset Hounds are quite capable of outsmarting their owners at almost every turn and take great delight in doing just that. That does not mean they're incapable of learning what you want them to learn. It simply means they will learn it on *their* terms rather than yours. You may find your dog to be conveniently deaf when it suits him.

Stubborn but extremely sensitive, a Basset takes harsh discipline to heart and will shut down and quit rather than comply when he is treated this way. Positive training methods work well, especially those involving small food treats.

My first experience training a Basset Hound to walk on a leash proved to me how different this breed really is. I tried a "make-him-do-it" method, jerking on the leash

Positive training with small food treats will be most successful with your Basset.

when the dog lagged behind me. He just fell farther behind, disgusted with my antics. Soon he was laid flat out on the ground like roadkill in a comic strip, and I could only drag him by the leash or give up. I had the sense to give up and try another, more motivating, method. Don't be surprised if your dog does this "Basset death roll" when you are trying to persuade him to obey a command he thinks is totally useless.

One key to success is establishing early on who is leading the pack known as the family. Never, under any circumstances, should the dog be the leader. Too often, owners of a cute little Basset Hound puppy (and they are the cutest pups) will let the four-legged youngster get away with all kinds of mischief, until it's too late.

You may think, "He's just a puppy; I can't correct him. Besides, he's so cute." Wrong. With any breed, if the discipline doesn't start from day one, you'll soon find that your darling puppy has become an unmanageable brat. He'll do only what *he* wants to do and may resort to aggression when you decide to take charge. By this time, he's no longer a small puppy but has matured into a large, strong dog. You'll have a major problem on your hands unless you get off to the right start with your pet.

Sports for Basset Hounds

For the serious competitor, there are more suitable breeds for dog sports. A Basset Hound can be an absolute embarrassment, not due to lack of intelligence or learning ability but because he's determined to do things by *his* rules. Equally strong is the Basset Hound's mission to entertain and amuse his audience at every opportunity.

Bassets enjoy agility, although they are not fast enough to win many trials.

In spite of all this, a Basset can excel with a patient and motivated trainer. Rally obedience, a relatively new AKC sport, allows the handler to encourage the dog in the ring, which a Basset loves. Agility is also a fun sport for a Basset Hound. Though not fast enough to win against some breeds his size, he can certainly hold his own and complete the obstacle course in the required time to qualify for a title. (For more information on obedience and other activities for you and your dog, see our bonus chapter at www.wiley.com/go/bassethound.)

Perhaps the most repeated Basset Hound obedience story—and one that is true—concerns a dog named George. He achieved his Companion Dog (CD) and Companion Dog Excellent (CDX) titles in AKC obedience, but hit a major snag when working toward his Utility Dog (UD) title. George quickly learned that he could become the center of attention and get lots of laughs if, instead of bringing back a glove on command, he returned to his owner with his *ear* in his mouth.

Once George devised this trick, there was no unlearning it. He kept it up until his frustrated owner retired him from competition and switched to an easier, less creative breed.

The Basset Hound's nose has also been known to create problems in the obedience ring. There are numerous stories about Bassets leaving the ring to befriend a spectator eating a hot dog at ringside.

The Basset Hound is a great dog, but is not the right pet for every family. Does everyone in your household agree that this is the right breed? If a Basset Hound sounds great to you, let's look at how to choose the perfect one for your family.

Chapter 4

Choosing Your Basset Hound

Every Basset Hound puppy is so cute that she's just about irresistible. Choosing one will be very difficult, but this chapter will give you some tips. Once you've selected your special puppy, it may be a week or two before you can bring her home. Even if you only have to wait a day, you have a lot to do in preparation for the big event. The next chapter will get you started.

Decisions to Make

You have several choices to consider when starting your search for the perfect pet. This is a decision you will be living with for the next twelve to fifteen years, so take your time and be sure you get the right dog for your family.

Male or Female?

When they're mature, females are a little smaller than males. Whether you prefer a male or female is largely a matter of personal taste, with one exception: If this will be your only dog, consider a female, especially if you are gone all day at work. Some people claim that males are more affectionate and females are more independent. I'm not sure this is true. But male Bassets do seem to suffer more from separation anxiety. (If you have a second dog in the family, of any breed, separation anxiety will not be as much of an issue.)

As puppies, all Basset Hounds are emotionally dependent—more so than other breeds. Puppies should stay with the litter until they are 10 to 12 weeks old. Before that, they are just too immature to be away from their mom and littermates.

Puppy or Adult?

With a puppy, you certainly get the cute stage. But you also have a lot of work ahead of you with housetraining and constant supervision. With an adult Basset Hound, especially if you work all day, your job is easier. The dog can be left alone for longer periods, and training issues won't be such a challenge. You know what the adult dog will look like, and any health problems will already be identified. You will also pay less for an adult dog. Adding a puppy will be like adding another child to the family; an adult dog may be easier for everyone.

Breeders often have young dogs they have kept for awhile to see how they turn out. Eventually, they decide some of these dogs are not right for the show ring and will place them in pet homes. Or they may have retired show dogs who are 5 or more years old. Most dogs available from rescue groups are also adults.

Re-homed Basset Hounds, especially in the 3-to-5-year age range, can be great pets for families with children. Don't think you have to get a puppy so the kids will grow up with her. Dogs are teenagers at 1 year old, way ahead of the kids. An adult is over the mouthy stage where she play-bites at everything that moves, including flailing arms and feet. An older dog realizes that the kids are not littermates and knows not to play too rough. However, you still have a responsibility to your children *and* the dog to monitor their interactions so everyone stays safe and each knows how to treat each other with care.

Yes, puppies are impossibly adorable, but adult dogs have many advantages.

One or Two?

I always recommend getting just one dog at a time, but if you decide to get two puppies, I recommend a male and a female, rather than two of the same sex. Opposite sexes are less likely to fight.

Littermates usually do not get the individual attention they need from their owners, and because they are never separated, the pups become overly dependent on one another as they grow up. You want your Basset Hound to be bonded with you and look to the people in the household as her pack. Wait six months and then get a second puppy.

Pet or Show Dog?

A pet-quality puppy from a reputable breeder probably has a very minor fault, like a crooked tooth or light-colored eyes, or will eventually be too tall to be shown. These puppies make great pets and grow into beautiful, sound adults. Pet puppies from show breeders are going to be carefully bred, with sound temperaments and the best structure possible.

A responsible breeder will sell a pet-quality puppy on a limited registration. With the limited registration, you will be entitled to receive registration papers, but any puppies your dog produces cannot be registered. The breeder may also have a clause in the contract that requires you to spay or neuter your puppy. You will still be able to compete with your altered Basset Hound in performance events like obedience and agility, if you want to.

If you think you want to show your dog, the breeder may want to retain co-ownership and mentor you as you learn about conformation shows. Most breeders will not sell a show prospect outright to a pet owner who has not shown before.

Consider a Rescued or Shelter Dog

Rescue organizations take in homeless dogs from shelters or owners and re-home them. These groups are usually run entirely by volunteers and are an excellent resource for adopting a Basset Hound.

Rescue groups in major cities may get a hundred or more Basset Hounds a year, so you will have plenty of dogs to choose from. Most don't get puppies, but they do get quite a few young dogs—Christmas puppies given up after the thrill has worn off, dogs from owners who didn't really know what they were getting into with a Basset, and dogs from animal shelters.

There are many wonderful dogs in shelters and rescue groups who just want to show you what a great pet they can be.

Don't think that all homeless Bassets were abused. Often neglected, yes, but not abused. Most dogs in shelters are there because they ran away and didn't have identification on them. They will still make great pets.

If you are unsure about the temperament of a shelter dog, working with a rescue group is a great way to find a Basset Hound. Often, the dog has lived for a time in a foster home. The volunteers are excellent matchmakers; they are experienced with the breed and know the individual Basset Hound well. Your Basset may even have been evaluated for compatibility with cats and children.

Adopted dogs have had health care and vaccinations, are spayed or neutered, and are flea-free when they go off to their new homes. Although you will pay a fee for a rescued dog, it will often be much less than you would have had to spend to rehabilitate her yourself. You will also get ongoing support from the organization and be able to return the dog if she doesn't work out.

Why do owners give up their Basset Hounds? Reasons vary, and people often don't tell the whole story when they relinquish a pet. But most homeless Basset Hounds adjust quickly and adore their new families. Rescue groups usually practice full disclosure, telling you what to expect in the way of behavior and health problems from your new dog.

The most common problem facing Basset Hounds who come into rescue is lack of care, such as toenails so long the dog can't walk or extreme obesity. Some dogs have had no training, or have been left alone too much and suffer from separation anxiety. With some attention and training, they shape up quickly.

Senior dogs are often available from rescue groups. These Bassets make wonderful pets, are sweet, mellow, and not overly active, and are so grateful to be a part of your family. You won't have your senior dog for as many years, but an older dog's health often improves dramatically with a little care, and she may live many more years than you originally expected.

> **TIP**
>
> Adoption is an excellent way to add a second dog to your home. If you get a Basset puppy, consider getting an adult as your second dog.

Where to Get a Puppy

Your best bet is to buy your Basset Hound puppy from a reputable breeder in your area. Buying from a breeder has several advantages. It is the best guarantee that your new puppy is a healthy, quality Basset. Quality is proven in the show ring, where dogs are evaluated for correct structure and soundness.

Responsible breeders have an enormous stake in every puppy they produce.

Breeders usually have years of experience with their breed and often have specific knowledge of common problems the breed encounters. Breeders also offer health guarantees and guidance on puppy care. A puppy you get from a nearby breeder will not have to endure the stress of being shipped across country or being separated from her littermates while she's still too young.

A puppy may not be readily available from your first choice of breeders. Responsible breeders plan their litters carefully; they don't breed just for Christmas or for the money. They are breeding to improve the Basset Hound breed, and they hope to get one or two show-quality puppies in every litter. Some will refer you to another breeder if they know of puppies available.

Responsible breeders have an enormous stake in every puppy they produce. Although you may have paid what you consider a hefty price for your pup, don't think the breeder got rich from the litter. The money spent on maintaining a healthy brood bitch, the stud fee, veterinary bills, food, and inoculations can never be recouped through puppy sales.

A breeder often supervises the litter twenty-four hours a day for the first three weeks. This may sound like overkill, but Basset Hounds can be notoriously clumsy climbing into and out of the whelping box, and pups are easily smothered or injured. With all this time and emotion invested in the babies, no wonder they want to do all they can to help you get off to a good start with your new family member. Most breeders hope you will keep in touch throughout the dog's life and are available to answer health and behavior questions.

Contact the Basset Hound Club of America (www.basset-bhca.org) or the American Kennel Club (www.akc.org) for a list of Basset Hound clubs and breeders in your area. If you end up on a waiting list for a puppy, rest assured the wait will be worth it.

How to Evaluate a Litter of Puppies

Another good reason to buy from a breeder is that you get to meet the pup's mother, often the father (or you will see a photo of him), and perhaps even the grandparents. This will give you a good idea of how your puppy will look and act as she matures.

Look at the mother and see if she is healthy, if she has any severe structural faults, and if she is friendly. A bitch (female dog) who won't let you near her or her pups has a poor temperament and will pass that along to her litter. This should be almost unheard of in a Basset Hound. The breeder should have been handling those puppies every day, and the mother should be used to it and allow it with no objections.

The puppies should be living in the breeder's home and interacting with a wide variety of people.

Have the puppies been raised in the home or out in a kennel? In the home, they'll get used to the sights and sounds of people, televisions, phones, and dishwashers. A well-socialized puppy will adjust quickly to your home. Are the facilities clean and well maintained? Dogs raised in filth will be harder to housetrain because they are used to relieving themselves where they sleep.

Watch how the pups interact with each other. You don't want to pick the shyest pup who is hiding in the corner. This shyness could be a problem later, resulting in a fear-biter when the overly shy puppy grows up. You don't want the rowdiest, most dominant puppy either, because this one may be *too* dominant. She could be harder to train and live with, especially for a first-time dog owner. Select a pup who is outgoing and friendly and allows you to handle her, settling down after a few seconds of squirming.

Health Issues to Look For

Ask the breeder about health problems in recent generations of their dogs and look at the pedigree of the litter you are considering. Are there any champions in the last three generations? If yes, this tells you this person is breeding only the best to the best.

Because the Basset Hound is a dwarf breed, structural defects are exaggerated and can result in a crippled dog. A dog with major faults should not be bred at all. Some problems you might see in poorly bred adult dogs include:

- Knuckled-over: the front knees are literally ahead of the feet, and in the worst cases, the front paws face almost backward
- Lack of breed "type": too tall, short ears, no wrinkles; starts to look like a Beagle
- Front legs not set under the dog properly: they can't support the dog's weight, which often causes arthritis
- Back problems: because the rib cage is too short or narrow and can't support the long back
- Glaucoma
- Skin problems: seborrhea, odor, or chronic yeast infections

A breeder should be able to describe the goals of their breeding program and be willing to answer your questions without hesitation. They also should offer a health guarantee against hereditary defects that may show up later in your dog.

The Basset Hound does not have many inherited health problems that can be identified before breeding. Just recently, genetic tests for von Willebrand's disease and thrombopathia have been developed, and some breeders are starting to screen to see if their dogs are carriers of these blood disorders. A carrier may not show symptoms, but could pass the disease on to the puppies if bred to another carrier. Learn more about the health problems that sometimes affect Basset Hounds in chapter 8.

Questions You'll Be Asked

Whether you get your new dog from a breeder or rescue organization, you will be interviewed. The breeder (or adoption counselor) wants their dogs to go to a permanent loving home that understands a Basset Hound and is willing to give her the type of care she needs. The perfect family is one that has owned Basset Hounds before, but there is a first time for everyone. If you grew up with Golden Retrievers, owning a Basset Hound will be a big adjustment, and the breeder wants to know that you understand what you are getting into.

Good breeders love to talk about their dogs and will be happy to see that you have done a lot of research and are asking a lot of questions. They will ask you about dogs you have had before, how long you had them, what health problems they had, and how you dealt with them. They will want to know where your new dog will sleep and spend her days, not just when she's a puppy, but when she grows up, too.

They will want to meet the entire family, including your children. A breeder will watch all of you interact with their adult dogs and puppies. Are you put off by all the drool? Are you fussy about getting dog hair on your clothes? Are you overly focused on the price? They want to know that you can afford to care for the dog throughout her life and that you have thought through the responsibilities of owning a Basset Hound.

After interviewing you, don't be surprised if the breeder offers you a choice between one or two pups they have selected as the best match for you. After all, they have lived with these pups every day for several months and know the personality of each one very well. Don't get too attached to a certain color or sex. Once you get your puppy home, she will be the most gorgeous puppy in the world within the first hour!

Basset Hound puppies usually go to their new homes when they are 10 to 12 weeks old. Your puppy will be more self-confident and better prepared to cope with unfamiliar things in her new home if she remains with her littermates until this age. By this time, the mother and siblings have taught her some puppy manners, like not to play too rough or bite so much. Letting the other puppies teach her is much faster than you trying to do it—though you will absolutely need to continue this training when you get her home.

Basset puppies need to stay with their mom and littermates until they are 10 to 12 weeks old.

Part II
Caring for Your Basset Hound

Chapter 5

Bringing Your Basset Hound Home

Now the fun begins! Get everything ready in advance for your new Basset Hound so his arrival will be stress-free for everyone.

Before the dog comes home, sit down with the family and decide who will be responsible for dog-care chores. Feeding, walking, and poop scooping can be split up and rotated among family members on different days. Realize that most of the work will fall to the parents. Children and teenagers get distracted with school, friends, and activities, and their interest in everyday care will wane as time goes by. It's great to teach your kids responsibility, but please don't do it at the dog's expense.

The box on page 43 lists the basics you'll need for your Basset Hound, puppy or adult. Consult with your dog's breeder before you select dog food. They will be able to tell you what works best for a Basset Hound puppy and what your puppy is used to eating.

Using a Crate

A crate is one of the most important purchases you'll ever make for your new hound. No one can watch a puppy every minute, and a dog crate is the most practical way to keep him safe and out of mischief. Puppy curiosity can tempt him to chew electrical wiring or taste toxic substances like antifreeze. None of these hazards will cross the path of a crated puppy or dog. Think of a crate as a playpen, not a jail.

Puppy Essentials

You'll need to go shopping *before* you bring your puppy home. There are many, many adorable and tempting items at pet supply stores, but these are the basics.

- **Food and water dishes.** Look for "hound" bowls that have narrow tops and wide bottoms, so your Basset Hound won't drag his ears through his food and water and then trail them all over your house. Stainless steel bowls are a good choice because they are easy to clean (plastic never gets completely clean) and almost impossible to break. Avoid bowls that place the food and water side by side in one unit—it's too easy for your dog to get his water dirty that way.
- **Leash.** A six-foot leather leash will be easy on your hands and very strong.
- **Collar.** Start with a nylon buckle collar. For a perfect fit, you should be able to insert two fingers between the collar and your pup's neck. Your dog will need larger collars as he grows up.
- **Crate.** Choose a sturdy crate that is easy to clean and large enough for your puppy to stand up, turn around, and lie down in.
- **Nail cutters.** Get a good, sharp pair that are the appropriate size for the nails you will be cutting. Your dog's breeder or veterinarian can give you some guidance here.
- **Grooming tools.** Different kinds of dogs need different kinds of grooming tools. See chapter 7 for advice on what to buy.
- **Chew toys.** Dogs *must* chew, especially puppies. Make sure you get things that won't break or crumble off in little bits, which the dog can choke on. Very hard plastic bones are a good choice. Dogs love rawhide bones, too, but pieces of the rawhide can get caught in your dog's throat, so they should only be allowed when you are there to supervise.
- **Toys.** Watch for sharp edges and unsafe items such as plastic eyes that can be swallowed. Many toys come with squeakers, which dogs can also tear out and swallow. All dogs will eventually destroy their toys; as each toy is torn apart, replace it with a new one.

In addition to safeguarding your puppy and your belongings, the crate is a useful housetraining tool and doubles as a den for your pet when he feels the need for privacy and quiet time. The dog is, after all, a den animal, and if the

A dog cannot spend all day in his crate. He needs to get out and have some fun.

crate is used properly, your pet will welcome the opportunity to retreat to it. Once accustomed to it, your dog will use it all his life. You'll often find him napping in his crate with the door open.

But, he cannot spend all day every day in his crate. An active, healthy dog needs exercise and interaction. The crate *never* should be used as punishment. Puppies should be let out after a short stay in the crate. Adult dogs can go several hours or overnight. Though some puppies or dogs might resist going in at first, a few well-placed treats will convince most rather quickly that this is a good place to be.

Put your Basset in his crate whenever he will be alone or unsupervised. When workers or visitors come to the house, he could escape through open doors or gates. If he is in his crate, you won't have to keep track of him. He will feel safe and will not feel the need to protect his territory.

> **TIP**
>
> Keep a crate in the bedroom so your Basset can sleep near you and one in the car so he can travel safely.

Your Basset Hound can ride safely in a crate when you travel by car. It's his home away from home in a hotel room or stranger's house. It will smell familiar and make him feel secure if you have to leave him alone for a few hours in a new place.

Selecting a Crate

The crate should be large enough that your dog can stand up and turn around. It should not be so large that it can be divided into a bedroom and a bathroom. Most dogs will not mess where they sleep, so don't give your Basset enough room to do both. A crate large enough for an adult can be divided with a barrier, so it can be lengthened as the puppy grows and requires additional room.

There are many kinds of crates. A wire one will keep him cool, and your pup won't feel as confined because he can watch the activities around him. If you need to, you can put a cloth over it to keep him warm or so he'll feel more protected. They also conveniently fold flat for storage.

Plastic crates are the only kind approved for airline travel and are not as drafty as wire. Canvas or fabric crates are lightweight and are easy to take with you, but can be torn apart by a dog who is not used to being crated. You can also buy beautiful wood crates that double as end tables and match the furniture in your home.

In addition to the crate, you may want to get an exercise pen (called *ex pen* for short) for your Basset Hound puppy. These wire pens confine your dog in a larger area than a crate and give him a little more freedom to move around. Ex pens work great at a picnic or while camping. If your pup learns to stay in a pen while he is still small, he won't be inclined to break out when he's bigger. An adult dog who is first introduced to an ex pen may be able to escape.

An exercise pen will keep your dog safe in outdoor areas that are not fenced.

Puppy-Proofing Your Home

You can prevent much of the destruction puppies can cause and keep your new dog safe by looking at your home and yard from a dog's point of view. Get down on all fours and look around. Do you see loose electrical wires, cords dangling from the blinds, or chewable shoes on the floor? Your pup will see them, too!

In the kitchen:

- Put all knives and other utensils away in drawers.
- Get a trash can with a tight-fitting lid.
- Put all household cleaners in cupboards that close securely; consider using childproof latches on the cabinet doors.

In the bathroom:

- Keep all household cleaners, medicines, vitamins, shampoos, bath products, perfumes, makeup, nail polish remover, and other personal products in cupboards that close securely; consider using childproof latches on the cabinet doors.
- Get a trash can with a tight-fitting lid.
- Don't use toilet bowl cleaners that release chemicals into the bowl every time you flush.
- Keep the toilet bowl lid down.
- Throw away potpourri and any solid air fresheners.

In the bedroom:

- Securely put away all potentially dangerous items, including medicines and medicine containers, vitamins and supplements, perfumes, and makeup.
- Put all your jewelry, barrettes, and hairpins in secure boxes.
- Pick up all socks, shoes, and other chewables.

In the rest of the house:

- Tape up or cover electrical cords; consider childproof covers for unused outlets.
- Knot or tie up any dangling cords from curtains, blinds, and the telephone.
- Securely put away all potentially dangerous items, including medicines and medicine containers, vitamins and supplements, cigarettes, cigars, pipes and pipe tobacco, pens, pencils, felt-tip markers, craft and sewing supplies, and laundry products.
- Put all houseplants out of reach.
- Move breakable items off low tables and shelves.
- Pick up all chewable items, including television and electronics remote controls, cell phones, MP3 players, shoes, socks, slippers and sandals, food, dishes, cups and utensils, toys, books and magazines, and anything else that can be chewed on.

In the garage:

- Store all gardening supplies and pool chemicals out of reach of the dog.
- Store all antifreeze, oil, and other car fluids securely, and clean up any spills by hosing them down for at least ten minutes.
- Put all dangerous substances on high shelves or in cupboards that close securely; consider using childproof latches on the cabinet doors.
- Pick up and put away all tools.
- Sweep the floor for nails and other small, sharp items.

In the yard:

- Put the gardening tools away after each use.
- Make sure the kids put away their toys when they're finished playing.
- Keep the pool covered or otherwise restrict your pup's access to it when you're not there to supervise.
- Secure the cords on backyard lights and other appliances.
- Inspect your fence thoroughly. If there are any gaps or holes in the fence, fix them.
- Make sure you have no toxic plants in the garden.

Toys

Ask your breeder to suggest some hound-proof toys for your Basset. Use caution and common sense when selecting playthings. Basset Hound teeth are sharp and their jaws are strong, so avoid soft rubber or toys with easily removable parts that can be swallowed.

When picking toys that squeak, make sure the squeaker can't be removed—and that your own ears can stand the sound. Some toys should be picked up and put away when you are not there to supervise. Because Bassets always love to eat, select a toy that occasionally dispenses a treat. It will entertain him for hours.

In addition to store-bought toys, favorite toys can be found right in your own home. Plastic soda or water bottles can provide entertainment by the hour for most puppies, and even for adult dogs. Stuffed toys (with the button eyes and nose removed) also make good companions for puppies, particularly at sleep time. They can be especially comforting when you first bring a pup home from the breeder.

Get a tag with your contact information to put on your puppy's collar.

Identification

Even though you have made sure your yard and home are secure, you still need to provide some identification for your dog. Accidents happen. A visitor could leave the gate open. Your dog could slip out of his collar and go chasing after a rabbit. If your Basset gets away, it is imperative that he have some form of identification or it is unlikely you will get him back.

Get an ID tag with your phone number on it to put on your puppy's collar when you pick him up to bring him home. The breeder may have already microchipped your puppy, but if not, plan to have your vet do it on your first visit. A microchip is a tiny numbered chip that is injected under your dog's skin between the shoulder blades. Shelters or vets can scan the chip with a reader and then trace the dog's owner through a microchip registry. You will need to register the microchip so the animal shelter can track you down. There is usually a one-time nominal fee to register the chip. Almost all animal shelters have scanners to read microchips.

In many areas, a dog license is mandatory. Consider it an insurance policy. With more than one form of identification, your chances of recovering a lost dog are increased dramatically.

Choosing a Name

One of the first things you will want to do when you pick your puppy is choose a name for him. Like babies, though, you don't know much about your puppy yet. You don't have much to go on except looks, so use your imagination. Just make sure it's a name that conveys your affection for your new puppy and one that you won't be embarrassed calling out across the park.

The important thing is not to change the name once you've chosen it. Don't use lots of cute nicknames because this confuses your puppy and just lengthens the time it takes for him to learn his real name. Use the name over and over

Many dogs have a formal name that's on their registration papers and what is known as a "call name"—what you really call the dog.

again. When you praise him and speak to him, look him right in the eyes and repeat it. Address him in a cheerful tone of voice and he will start responding to his new name quickly.

Your dog's breeder may want you to include the kennel name on your puppy's registration papers. You can choose something elegant or fun after the kennel name. If the kennel name was Windmill Basset Hounds, you could choose something like Windmill Don Quixote for the name. What you call your dog every day may have nothing to do with his registered name. It is entirely up to you.

Bringing Your Puppy Home

Now the fun begins! The day you pick up your puppy, the breeder will send you home with lots of information about vaccinations, feeding, worming, and training. You should get information about what shots the puppy has had and when he will need boosters, and when he was wormed and when he should be wormed again.

The breeder may send you home with a supply of puppy food to help prevent stomach upsets during the transition. Ask for a towel or blanket that has the mother's and littermates' smell on it so your pup won't be frightened the first night in his new home. You should get his AKC registration papers the day you pick him up. If the pup has been microchipped, you will get the forms to register with the proper agency.

The First Day and Night

This is the first time your Basset Hound puppy has ever been away from his mother and littermates for any period of time. The new surroundings of your home will be unfamiliar, and you can expect your puppy to be a little worried at first. His first night in your home may not be the most peaceful.

Take the puppy outside as soon as you arrive home. Let him sniff and go potty (in a place you have chosen in advance). Don't overwhelm him with too much attention. Just stand back and watch while he explores. Children and other pets should be

> **TIP**
>
> Basset Hounds are built low to the ground, and some aren't too fond of dragging their private parts through wet grass and snow in the winter. If your dog suffers a housetraining relapse when the weather changes, consider setting up a dry spot under cover, surfaced with gravel or shavings, to make your hound's trip outside more pleasant.

introduced quietly, one at a time, so the pup isn't overly intimidated. You want this to be a positive experience.

Adequate rest is absolutely essential for a young puppy. Puppies play full blast and then collapse for a long nap. Then they wake up and play hard, eat, and nap again. Don't let excited children and their friends overtire him. Be sure he gets a nap or two, even on his first day.

At bedtime, put your puppy to bed in his crate with lots of soft blankets, including the blanket or towel you brought home with his littermates' scent on it. Keep the crate in your room so he can be comforted by your closeness. Do not take him out when he starts to cry, but do offer him reassuring

Give your pup a blanket and a toy in his crate.

words and let him know you are nearby. Some people suggest wrapping a ticking clock in a blanket and putting it in the puppy's crate; this simulates the mother's heartbeat and can help calm the puppy down. He will sleep for a few hours and will probably need to go out once or twice during the night.

The First Few Weeks

I hope you will be able to spend a day or two with your Basset Hound before you have to leave him and go to work all day. Bassets are prone to separation anxiety, and during his first days in his new home he will be looking for his pack members. It's a great time for him to start bonding to you and the family—his new pack.

Set up a spot on hard flooring, not carpet, where you can safely leave your puppy for a few hours. A laundry room, kitchen, or other small area works best. Your puppy can't handle the responsibility of being loose in a large room yet. If you bought an ex pen, this is an excellent opportunity to use it. Or, you can block a door with baby gates to confine him. Set up food, water, toys, and a bed at one end, and some newspapers or puppy piddle-pads at the other. Assume he will have some accidents the first few weeks.

Make time for your new Basset Hound so he can start to bond with his new family.

Consider hiring a pet sitter to come in and give your puppy a midday meal and potty break. Housetraining will take a little longer if you are unable to be at home with him during the day.

A Schedule for You and Your Puppy

Establish a schedule on the first day and stick to it as much as possible. Your Basset Hound will feel more secure if he knows when he will be fed and walked, when he'll be let out, and what time his family will be home.

When you are setting up your puppy's schedule, consider the family's timetable: what time people are at home to play with the puppy, when family members get home from work, when they leave in the morning, and what other obligations they have in the evenings. If family members usually wake up at seven and leave the house at eight, someone will have to start waking up earlier to walk, feed, and pay attention to the puppy.

Children and Your Puppy

Kids and dogs naturally belong together. But they don't automatically know how to play with each other safely. With a little guidance from parents, children can help with daily dog-care chores, participate in training, and become lifelong friends with their dog. When both puppy and child know the rules and treat each other with respect, they will form a wonderful bond.

Never leave an infant or toddler alone with a dog or puppy. Once a child is old enough to understand, teach them how to play games with the dog. Tug-of-war can lead to aggression and possessiveness, so this game is off-limits. Teach them how to be gentle with a dog and not to poke eyes, ears, and other sensitive areas.

Don't allow your children to pick up the puppy. Basset Hounds, even puppies, are too heavy and awkward for a child to lift. Their long backs can be easily injured.

Play-Biting and Jumping

When planning your puppy's entertainment, realize it's a very short step between play and aggression, and rough games can lead to undesirable biting behavior. All puppies play-bite, but biting should never be tolerated. No matter how cute it seems at the moment, always keep in mind that your puppy will end up a sixty-plus-pound dog with sharp teeth and strong jaws. If you let him nip as a puppy, he has no way of learning when to stop.

Your puppy needs to be introduced to as many people, animals, and situations as possible. This process is called socialization.

Many a dog has ended up in a shelter for biting family members who at one time thought this behavior was cute. When your Basset puppy puts his mouth on you, whether chewing or biting, yelp "Ow!" loudly and walk away, ending the game. This is how his littermates would tell him he has bitten too hard.

Teach children that jumping around and waving their arms encourages a puppy to jump and bite. If the pup gets too excited, have your children hug themselves with both arms, turn away, and stand still to help calm the puppy. Praise the puppy quietly when he stops misbehaving.

Kids and dogs will naturally get overexcited while playing. When games get too rough, give your Basset Hound a time-out in the crate. This gives him and the children a chance to settle down.

Beginning Training and Socialization

Your veterinarian will tell you when it is safe to take your puppy out into the wide world. Until your puppy has completed his shots, he is very susceptible to parvovirus, distemper, and other life-threatening diseases. Save the dog park until he is older.

Socialization is crucial in a puppy's first six months. Your dog needs to meet kids, senior citizens, and dogs and cats, and visit lots of different places. He needs to see raincoats and umbrellas, motorcycles and cars, asphalt and grass, gravel and dirt. People in uniform, in wheelchairs, and on skateboards are all new to your Basset Hound. Even a visit to the vet is an opportunity to socialize your puppy. Take him in so he can get a treat and be admired by everyone, rather than poked and prodded.

Basset Hounds are slow to mature. This is one reason why breeders usually keep Basset puppies with their littermates longer than some other breeds. Positive experiences are critical at this age. Don't let your dog be terrified by loud noises, sudden commotion, or things he hasn't seen before. His fear might remain throughout his life. An overly timid puppy can grow up into a dog who bites when he is afraid. Let him encounter scary things from a distance and don't comfort him if he shows fear. Speak in an upbeat, happy tone and let him explore new things when he is ready, without forcing him.

Puppy Kindergarten

Puppies have a very short attention span, so make training sessions quick and fun—less than five minutes. Whether you think you are playing or training, your puppy is always learning, so start setting the rules the first day he arrives. Especially, no jumping and no biting. Don't wait until your dog is a year old to

Finding a Trainer

Nothing beats a personal recommendation. Ask your dog's breeder, veterinarian, people at the dog park, friends, and neighbors about obedience classes in your area. Also check at the local pet supply store and boarding kennel for recommendations. Park and recreation departments or the local shelter may offer classes in your city. The Internet is a great place to find out more about local obedience and puppy classes, too.

Once you have located a trainer you are interested in, ask if you can come and watch a class without your puppy. See if you like the instructors' methods. Do they answer questions from students? Do they seem to genuinely like the dogs and people? Are the classes small enough to give students individual attention? Is everyone having fun? Can the whole family attend?

It will be hard to find a trainer who personally owns Basset Hounds, but your teacher should be familiar with the breed and have had some Bassets in previous classes. Not all dogs can be trained using the same method. Bassets don't respond in the same way and aren't motivated by the same things as other breeds. Basset Hounds are far from stupid, and you don't want an instructor who thinks they are.

start training! Puppies learn quickly and what they learn will stick with them for life.

Once his puppy shots are completed, the best way to start training and socialization is to take your dog to a puppy class. The entire family should attend classes so you all are consistent in training your puppy. Your Basset Hound will be introduced to basic obedience and learn dog manners by playing with dogs close to his own age.

An adult Basset Hound can be really stubborn, so early training paves the way for cooperation. After completing puppy class, continue with a basic obedience class as soon as he is old enough. Dog trainers establish a minimum age for

Keep training sessions short and positive, and your puppy will love to learn.

basic classes, usually when the dog is 4 to 6 months old.

As your puppy matures, he will go through stages where he appears to have forgotten everything you've taught him. Be patient and continue working with him until he "recovers" his memory. Just like human teenagers, he will test you to see what he can get away with. Even the most stubborn Basset Hound will ultimately give in and do your bidding, but only if you are equally stubborn and refuse to let him have his way!

Following these basic tips should get you off to a good start and provide you with the foundation you need to establish a long-term, loving relationship with your beautiful hound.

Chapter 6

Feeding Your Basset Hound

Basset Hounds are notorious eaters and gain weight easily. In spite of this, you'll be glad to hear that it is not that difficult to feed your hound properly and keep her healthy.

Above all, remember that your dog is just that—a *dog*. She will not get bored as people do with the same meal over and over again. You do not need to cook for her (except perhaps when she is ill) and you certainly don't need a variety of dog foods filling up your cupboards. Stick with one top-quality dog food and you'll be repaid many times over with a well-conditioned, healthy animal.

Feeding Puppies

When you pick up your puppy from the breeder, you should receive instructions on the feeding schedule, the brand, and the amount of food to feed her. Puppies will wolf down their food, so if you're feeding a dry kibble, moisten it to prevent choking. If you decide to change to another brand, make the transition gradually, adding a small amount of the new food to each meal until you have switched over a period of four or five days. A sudden switch may cause diarrhea.

Your dog's breeder will tell you whether your puppy is eating three or four meals a day. Puppies require more food than adults because of the additional demands of growth and their high activity level, but they also have smaller tummies. Three meals daily are advisable until at least 5 months of age, although many people continue the three-a-day schedule until the pup is 6 to 8 months old. At this age, cut back to two a day and switch to adult food.

Growing puppies and adult dogs have different nutritional needs. Puppies need puppy food.

Strong bones are so important for Basset Hounds that many breeders recommend you supplement puppy food with a little bit of calcium-rich goat's milk, cottage cheese, or evaporated milk. Use a very small amount—just enough to moisten the food. Too much will cause diarrhea.

Feeding Adult Dogs

Individual adult dogs vary in how much they should eat to maintain a desired body weight—not too fat, but not too thin. Determine how much food keeps your adult dog looking and feeling her best based on her size and activity level. If you follow the instructions on the pet food bag, you will probably feed too much. Two to three cups of dry food a day is about average for an adult Basset Hound. If you're worried about overfeeding, make sure you measure carefully and resist adding table scraps to the meals. Monitor your dog's weight and adjust her food accordingly.

Leave your dog's food out only for the amount of time it takes her to eat it—ten minutes, for example. Free feeding (when food is available all the time) encourages picky eating. If she doesn't finish her meal, pick it up and don't offer her anything else until her next mealtime. This will keep your dog in good weight. It will also help her recognize you as the keeper of the food, making you the pack leader in her eyes.

Follow a regular feeding schedule and try to feed your dog at the same times every day. Dogs are more secure about their place in the pack if they can count on a regular schedule for their activities, including meals.

Risk of Bloat

Although many breeds do well on one meal a day, because the Basset Hound is a high-risk breed for bloat, experts recommend two meals a day. Bloat (also known as gastric torsion) is an often fatal, always dangerous digestive problem that occurs primarily in deep-chested dogs. The stomach fills with gas and then twists, so it has no outlet. If the problem is not detected and dealt with immediately, the dog can die.

If you suspect bloat, take your dog to the vet immediately; it is a life-threatening emergency. Signs include a hard, swollen abdomen, attempts to vomit, pacing, and obvious distress.

Bloat is thought to have several causes. Eating or drinking too much too fast makes a dog gulp air with her food and causes excess gas. Feeding two or more meals a day means each meal is smaller, which helps prevent bloat. A dog who eats only one meal will be stressed due to hunger and more likely to gobble her food as well. Moisten the food with a little water and let it soak for about twenty minutes so it will expand in the bowl, not in her stomach.

Breeds with a broad, deep chest, such as Basset Hounds, are prone to bloat—a health problem related to eating. Feeding several meals a day helps prevent it.

Too much exercise before or after meals is thought to be another contributor to this dangerous condition. Enforce a rest period of about a half hour before and after meals to help digestion. My own dogs typically are fed in their crates and forced to have quiet time before and after their meals. I'll talk more about bloat in chapter 8.

Feeding Senior Dogs

As your dog ages, she will not be as active and won't need as much food. A Basset Hound is considered a senior dog by 8 years old. If she is not active or is overweight, you could consider her a senior as young as 6 years. Your vet can advise you when it is time to call your Basset a senior citizen.

Switch her to a diet formulated especially for older dogs, which will contain less calories and additional fiber to aid digestion. Other ingredient percentages may be adjusted as well. Many dog food companies add supplements like glucosamine and chondroitin to help prevent arthritic changes. You can also add the supplements yourself to your dog's diet. Check the ingredients before you add your own supplements, so you don't over-supplement your old dog.

What to Feed Your Basset Hound

Dog food manufacturers spend millions of dollars testing and determining optimum levels of nutrients for dogs in different life phases. Unless your dog is ill or recuperating and is off her usual food, it's easiest for you and healthiest for your dog to stick with commercial food.

Your Basset needs protein, carbohydrates, fats, vitamins, and minerals in the right proportions to remain healthy and fit. If you are feeding a high-quality dog food, all these things should be present in the correct amounts.

When you check out the dog food section at the store, there are so many different brands, formulas, flavors, and types of food that it's hard to know what to choose. Use the following information and the recommendations of your dog's breeder and vet to choose foods that will keep your Basset in peak condition throughout her life.

> **TIP**
> Always, always have fresh water available for your dog. Check the water bowl at least twice a day to make sure she has a good supply. Change the water and thoroughly rinse the bowl daily. If your dog will be outside, make sure she also has access to clean water there.

Dry Food (Kibble)

Nutritionally complete dry food is the main component of most canine diets. Choose a high-quality brand (available from pet supply stores) and select the formula that is appropriate for your dog's age and activity level. Less expensive brands sometimes substitute substandard ingredients, dyes, and fillers that can cause health problems. You will need to feed less of a high-quality food because it is more digestible, so it is worth spending a little more for it.

Raw and Homemade Food

Indoors and out, always have fresh water available for your dog.

Raw diets, known as BARF (bones and raw food), are becoming increasingly popular. If you are interested in preparing special meals for your dog, do your homework because you can easily do more harm than good. Work with a trusted veterinarian or canine nutritionist who specializes in natural diets. You will need to plan carefully to include the proper balance of protein, vitamins, minerals, and carbohydrates so that your dog doesn't develop dangerous deficiencies. Feeding a raw or homemade diet can be successful if you are willing to devote the time and money to doing it right.

If It Works, Stick with It

Basset Hounds are easy keepers, meaning they don't often need a special diet. If your dog has a nice coat, is a good weight, and appears to be in good health overall, there is no need to switch to a homemade diet or a commercial food filled with exotic ingredients. Good commercial adult maintenance formulas meet the needs of most dogs.

Read the dog food labels carefully and choose a food with plenty of protein from meat sources.

Remember that dogs are meat-eaters and need animal protein in their daily diet. Don't try to make your Basset Hound a vegetarian.

Do not feed cooked bones to your dog. A Basset Hound's strong teeth can splinter the brittle bones, and she'll swallow the pieces, which could puncture the intestines or bowels.

Canned Food

Canned food is more expensive than dry food and contains up to 70 percent water. Some canned foods are not nutritionally complete, so make sure you read the label. If it does not say "complete" or "nutritionally complete," it is not enough to provide a healthy diet on its own.

Because canned food is soft and moist, it does not help clean your dog's teeth or massage her gums. Remember to refrigerate canned food once it has been opened.

Semimoist Food

Semimoist food is often colored and packaged to look like hamburgers. This means nothing to the dog and is designed to attract the owner, who is doing the shopping. Semimoist foods tend to have large amounts of sugar, salt, artificial colorings, and preservatives, none of which your dog needs. If you choose to feed this kind of food to your dog, consider offering small bits as a treat rather than feeding large quantities as a meal.

Snacks and Treats

Dry dog biscuits are useful as treats between meals or during training sessions. Hard biscuits are good for your dog's teeth and help control tartar. A great way to entertain your Basset when you leave home is to get a treat-dispensing ball and put her meal or snack in it.

When you are adding up your dog's daily caloric intake, don't forget to count the treats. Basset Hounds are prone to obesity, so keep goodies to a minimum. Offer little tidbits—a small piece of biscuit instead of the whole thing. Other healthy treats you can feed your dog include bits of fruit or vegetables, like apple slices or carrots.

In addition to treats, dogs need to chew. Heavy-duty Nylabones or Galileo Bones can usually withstand a determined chewer. Pressed rawhide seems to be safer for Basset Hounds than other kinds. Whatever kind of bones you give your dog, supervise her and remove the bone if she starts to break off pieces that could be swallowed.

Fresh vegetables make great dog treats.

Vitamins and Supplements

More of a good thing is not necessarily better. Too many vitamins and minerals, just like too few, can result in dangerous health problems. In fact, a growing puppy is in danger of developing musculoskeletal disorders by oversupplementation. If your veterinarian prescribes a certain supplement for a specific condition, follow their advice. Otherwise, save your money.

Reading Dog Food Labels

Dog food labels are not always easy to read, but if you know what to look for they can tell you a lot about what your dog is eating.

- The label should have a statement saying the dog food meets or exceeds the American Association of Feed Control Officials (AAFCO) nutritional guidelines. If the dog food doesn't meet AAFCO guidelines, it can't be considered complete and balanced, and can cause nutritional deficiencies.
- The guaranteed analysis lists the minimum percentages of crude protein and crude fat and the maximum percentages of crude fiber and water. AAFCO requires a minimum of 18 percent crude protein for adult dogs and 22 percent crude protein for puppies on a dry matter basis (that means with the water removed; canned foods will have less protein because they have more water). Dog food must also have a minimum of 5 percent crude fat for adults and 8 percent crude fat for puppies.
- The ingredients list the most common item in the food first, and so on until you get to the least common item, which is listed last.
- Look for a dog food that lists an animal protein source first, such as chicken or poultry meal, beef or beef byproducts, and that has other protein sources listed among the top five ingredients. That's because a food that lists chicken, wheat, wheat gluten, corn, and wheat fiber as the first five ingredients has more chicken than wheat, but may not have more chicken than all the grain products put together.
- Other ingredients may include a carbohydrate source, fat, vitamins and minerals, preservatives, fiber, and sometimes other additives purported to be healthy.
- Some brands may add artificial colors, sugar, and fillers—all of which should be avoided.

The Overweight Basset Hound

Basset Hounds will eat until they die. A roly-poly puppy may be cute, but she's also a health disaster waiting to happen. The bone structure of the Basset

Hound cannot carry too much weight without permanent damage. An obese adult Basset risks heart disease, back problems, and myriad other health problems. Extra weight on the young Basset Hound will stress the short leg bones and possibly cause permanent limb problems.

If your dog gets too heavy, adjust the amount you feed her. Regardless of how much someone recommends, if your dog is too fat, then she is eating too much! A Basset Hound should have a bit of a waist behind her rib cage, and you should be able to feel her ribs as you run your hands down her sides. Her ribs shouldn't be too obvious, but you should at least be able to find them.

If you're still not sure, a visit to your dog's breeder or veterinarian may be in order. If they tell you the dog is overweight, don't take it personally. Accept the news as being in your Basset Hound's best interest and try to make the recommended diet changes.

Most of the quality pet food manufacturers include a low-calorie or "light" food. Veterinarians also sell low-calorie prescription dog foods. When your Basset Hound goes on a diet, you'll need to cut back on treats, too. At a normal weight, a limited number of biscuits or other treats is fine. The dieting dog need not be deprived. Try small pieces of raw carrot or apple, switch to low-calorie biscuits and break them into small pieces, or just give a couple of kernels of the dog's regular diet kibble as a treat. *What* you give matters little to the dog.

Most Bassets will eat until they burst. And it's tough for an overweight Basset to slim down. To keep your dog fit and active, pay attention to how much you feed her.

Pet Food vs. People Food

Many of the foods we eat are excellent sources of nutrients—after all, we do just fine on them. But dogs, like us, need the right combination of meat and other ingredients for a complete and balanced diet, and a bowl of meat doesn't provide that. In the wild, dogs eat the fur, skin, bones, and guts of their prey, and even the contents of the stomach.

This doesn't mean your dog can't eat what you eat. A little meat, dairy, bread, some fruits, or vegetables as a treat are great. Just remember, we're talking about the same food you eat, not the gristly, greasy leftovers you would normally toss in the trash. Stay away from sugar, too, and remember that chocolate and alcohol are toxic to dogs.

If you want to share your food with your dog, be sure the total amount you give her each day doesn't make up more than 15 percent of her diet, and that the rest of what you feed her is a top-quality complete and balanced dog food. (More people food could upset the balance of nutrients in the commercial food.)

Can your dog eat an entirely homemade diet? Certainly, if you are willing to work at it. Any homemade diet will have to be carefully balanced, with all the right nutrients in just the right amounts. It requires a lot of research to make a proper homemade diet, but it can be done. It's best to work with a veterinary nutritionist.

Picky Eaters

Although most Basset Hounds are not finicky eaters, some do learn that by turning up their noses at their dog food, concerned owners will break out the treats or table scraps. Unless you want sad eyes gazing up at you and a wet mouth on your knee every time the family sits down to a meal, limit your pet to her own food in her own dish at her own mealtime.

Although it's difficult to watch your Basset walk away from a full dish, keep in mind that a healthy dog will not starve herself to death. In nature, it is not unheard for an animal to just skip a meal. Give her a few minutes to eat and then pick up the dish. Repeat the routine at the next mealtime and keep repeating it until your dog gets the message and settles for her dog food. Once you give in and add the table scraps she's begging for, she'll have you trained for life.

If you honestly feel you must entice your dog to eat, try mixing in some cottage cheese, garlic powder, or even a spoonful of canned food. At the same time, you should know your dog's attitude and appearance well enough to distinguish between a finicky eater who's trying to hold

Don't let your dog teach you to be constantly spicing up her meal selections. Stick with healthy, wholesome foods and she will eat them.

out for people food and a sick pet. If your Basset Hound acts sluggish, has runny eyes, feels warm to the touch, or seems abnormal in any way, it may be time to visit the veterinarian. On the other hand, if her attitude and appearance are perfectly normal, wait her out. Chances are she'll return to eating her dog food once she's convinced that nothing else is coming her way.

Poisonous Foods

Some foods are definitely taboo for dogs. Heading this list is chocolate, which is toxic to dogs and should be avoided at all times. Holidays are particularly dangerous, especially Christmas, Valentine's Day, Easter, and Halloween, when candy seems to be all over the house. Children should be warned and watched carefully to make sure they don't leave their chocolate Easter bunnies within reach. If your dog eats some chocolate, call your veterinarian immediately so you know what precautions to take and what poisoning symptoms to look for.

Other people foods that are dangerous to dogs include alcohol, coffee, onions, raisins, grapes, and food sweetened with the artificial sweetener xylitol.

Chapter 7

Grooming Your Basset Hound

Basset Hounds are wash-and-wear dogs and require only a minimum amount of grooming. However, they do need *some* maintenance. Without it, they soon become an unattractive source of offensive odor and dirt.

Grooming Supplies

You won't need many grooming supplies, thanks to the Basset Hound's short coat. However, that coat does shed a lot. A short weekly cleanup session with a few tools will considerably reduce the number of baths required to keep your hound clean.

Your grooming kit should include a rubber currycomb, shedding blade, grooming glove, nail clippers, toothbrush and toothpaste for dogs, ear cleaner, and cotton swabs.

A bristle brush, like a hairbrush for humans, only removes surface hair. A rubber currycomb is more effective, especially when your dog is shedding. Bassets will shed heavily once or twice a year. The curry comb fits in your hand and has knobs that massage the dog's hair and skin. Move it in a circular motion deep into the coat, which brings lots of loose hair and dirt to the surface. Your dog will enjoy the sensation.

A shedding blade is a metal strip with a serrated edge that you rake over the top of the coat. In addition to removing a lot of dead hair, it also picks up all the hair the currycomb brought to the surface.

A shedding blade will remove dead hair along the surface of the coat.

A grooming glove fits on your hand like a regular glove. It has little bumps on it that remove loose surface hair and dirt as you wipe it over the dog's coat. When you have finished with the other tools, the glove removes the last remaining loose matter and leaves the coat shiny and clean looking. The glove is also great for touch-ups between grooming sessions.

Bath Time

Most Bassets love sloshing through every mud puddle they find, and will need an occasional bath. The underside of that low-slung body attracts dirt like a magnet.

When it's bath time, put on your oldest clothes and get out lots of old towels. On a warm day, an outdoor bath is a cool treat for both of you. Indoors, a walk-in shower with a handheld shower spray is the easiest way to bathe your dog.

If you're lifting your dog into a tub without help, place his front feet on the edge of the tub and gently boost the rest of him in while supporting his front with one hand on his chest. If you have assistance, one

> **TIP**
>
> Keep some waterless spray shampoo on hand for a quick and easy cleanup between baths.

New Products in the Fight Against Fleas

At one time, battling fleas meant exposing your dog and yourself to toxic dips, sprays, powders, and collars. But today there are flea preventives that work very well and are safe for your dog, you, and the environment. The two most common types are insect growth regulators (IGRs), which stop the immature flea from developing or maturing, and adult flea killers. To deal with an active infestation, experts usually recommend a product that has both.

These next-generation flea fighters generally come in one of two forms:

- **Topical treatments or spot-ons.** These products are applied to the skin, usually between the shoulder blades. The product is absorbed through the skin into the dog's system.
- **Systemic products.** This is a pill your dog swallows that transmits a chemical throughout the dog's bloodstream. When a flea bites the dog, it picks up this chemical, which then prevents the flea's eggs from developing.

Talk to your veterinarian about which product is best for your dog. Make sure you read all the labels and apply the products exactly as recommended, and that you check to make sure they are safe for puppies.

person can pick up the front end while the other lifts the rear to place the dog gently in the tub.

A spray nozzle attached to the faucet makes it easy to wet the dog down thoroughly. If you don't have a spray, use a large paper cup or plastic container to wet him with warm (not hot) water. Avoid using a glass container because when the dog suddenly shakes himself, he could knock it out of your hand and broken glass will go everywhere.

A plastic hook or ring attached to the wall will give you an anchor for a grooming noose, a leashlike restraint that keeps the dog in the tub and leaves your hands free. Available from most pet supply stores, the noose holds your Basset steady and under control during the bath.

Purchase a good-quality shampoo made for dogs. Shampoo for humans is too harsh and will dry out your dog's skin and coat. There are a number of rinses, conditioners, and other coat products on the market, but the Basset Hound seldom needs these extras. What he might need, however, is a non-chemical odor-eater in the rinse water to eliminate the hound smell. For Basset Hounds with skin problems, your veterinarian can recommend a good medicated shampoo.

One soaping, followed by thorough rinsing, will clean the average dog. While your dog is in the tub, be sure to clean the ears and check for any ticks, especially during the summer months. Favorite hiding spots are in the ears, on the neck, and between the toes. If you find one, remove it as described in the box on page 72.

After toweling your dog off as much as possible, you have several options, depending on the weather. On a warm, sunny day, you can take your Basset outside to run around and dry off. Make sure there are no convenient mud puddles or you'll be starting the whole process over again!

In wet or cold weather, your dog should be kept indoors until he's dry. You can use a hair dryer to speed the process.

Always carefully dry the wrinkles in your dog's face to prevent infections.

How to Get Rid of a Tick

Although many of the new generation of flea fighters are partially effective in killing ticks once they are on your dog, they are not 100 percent effective and will not keep ticks from biting your dog in the first place. During tick season (which, depending on where you live, can be spring, summer, and/or fall), examine your dog every day for ticks. Pay particular attention to your dog's neck, behind the ears, the armpits, and the groin.

When you find a tick, use a pair of tweezers to grasp the tick as close as possible to the dog's skin and pull it out using firm, steady pressure. Check to make sure you get the whole tick (mouth parts left in your dog's skin can cause an infection), then wash the wound and dab it with a little antibiotic ointment. Watch for signs of inflammation.

Ticks carry very serious diseases that are transmittable to humans, so dispose of the tick safely. *Never* crush it between your fingers. Don't flush it down the toilet either, because the tick will survive the trip and infect another animal. Instead, use the tweezers to place the tick in a tight-sealing jar or plastic dish with a little alcohol, put on the lid, and dispose of the container in an outdoor garbage can. Wash the tweezers thoroughly with hot water and alcohol.

Whether the dog dries outdoors or indoors, use a towel to dry his face wrinkles, ears, and feet. These areas, if left damp, are prone to yeast infections and other skin problems, so it is especially important to get them completely dry.

A good bath will loosen up the hair that's ready to fall out, so if you ignore the next step in the grooming process, you're asking for a house full of dog hair. Once your dog is thoroughly dry, it's time to get out the currycomb or shedding blade and get rid of the loose coat and dead skin. This also is the appropriate time to trim toenails.

Nail Trimming

Teach your dog from puppyhood to allow you to handle his feet and cut his toe-nails without a fuss. Regular, gentle handling of a puppy's feet and matter-of-fact nail clipping should result in a well-mannered dog who accepts this kind of attention.

If nail cutting is accompanied by lots of anxious, apologetic soothing from you, the puppy will grow up believing this is a horrible experience, and it will be—for both of you. I teach my dogs to cooperate by giving them a tiny treat after I cut each nail. They line up in front of me with a paw in the air on Sunday nights when I get the clippers out!

When cutting the nails, start with the back feet and you'll be halfway through before your dog even knows what you're doing. Be careful to avoid the quick, the little bundle of nerves and blood vessels that runs down the center of each nail. It hurts if you cut it. This pale red core is easier to see on white toenails. When in doubt, cut just the tiniest bit of the tip off. Trim several times a week to work long nails back to a safe length.

If a Basset Hound's nails are allowed to grow too long, it can affect his ability to walk by changing the alignment of his legs and joints. If you can't clip the nails yourself, take him to a vet or groomer and have it done. This is too important to neglect. Volunteers from rescue groups tell me that the biggest problem Basset Hounds coming into rescue have is crippled legs caused by long toenails.

In addition to cutting the nails, check the pads of the feet to make sure there are no ticks, cuts, or sores.

Overgrown nails are a real problem in this breed. Get in the habit of regularly trimming your dog's nails.

Ear Cleaning

Clean your dog's ears at least once a week with a cotton ball and warm water or veterinary ear cleaning solution. This will help ward off painful, smelly, and potentially costly ear infections. Basset Hound ears are long and heavy—a perfect breeding ground for bacteria and yeast. Moisture or dirt left in the ears increases the risk of infection.

Just clean as far as you can easily see and reach. Don't stick anything down into the ear canal; you might puncture an eardrum. Leave the deepest cleaning to your vet.

If your Basset Hound is shaking his head or scratching his ears, it's a sure sign you've not been keeping up with ear cleaning. Once this starts, a visit to the veterinarian is inevitable.

Teeth Cleaning

Maintaining your Basset Hound's teeth will help minimize the risk of bad breath, gum disease, and infection that could spread throughout his body. Your veterinarian or the dog's breeder can show you how to brush your pet's teeth. Not only will this keep your dog's teeth in top-notch shape, it ultimately will save you money on expensive veterinary bills for dental work.

Start teaching him early and your dog will learn to accept having his teeth brushed.

Doggie toothpaste tastes great (to a dog!), and he will learn to enjoy the process. Never use human toothpaste; it can make your hound sick.

Skin Check

Grooming time is also an opportunity to check your pet for fleas, ticks, and other skin problems. Fleas make your dog itch, causing hot spots, infection, and hair loss. As the fleas spread from pet to pet, you'll get bitten, too.

Look for live fleas and flea dirt—black specks (droppings) or white specks (eggs)—at the roots of your pet's hair, down by the skin. Most often, you'll see flea dirt on your dog's tummy and at the base of the tail.

Hot spots are painful patches of red skin that appear suddenly and can expand to several inches across as the dog scratches to relieve the irritation. Basset Hounds are most prone to hot spots in areas where moisture tends to accumulate, such as under the chin and on the feet, legs, and wherever there are skin folds.

To prevent hot spots, keep your Basset's wrinkles dry and clean. Hot spots can also occur when your dog scratches because of fleas, ear problems, allergies, or impacted anal glands.

An antiseptic powder, available from your veterinarian, will usually dry the hot spots and promote healing. If they go untreated for any length of time, the

Check your dog's skin carefully after each outing for ticks, awns (seed heads), foxtails, and other things that could hurt him.

Making Your Environment Flea Free

If there are fleas on your dog, there are fleas in your home, yard, and car, even if you can't see them. Take these steps to combat them.

In your home:

- Wash whatever is washable (the dog bed, sheets, blankets, pillow covers, slipcovers, curtains, etc.).
- Vacuum everything else in your home—furniture, floors, rugs, everything. Pay special attention to the folds and crevices in upholstery, the cracks between floorboards, and the spaces between the floor and the baseboards. Flea larvae are sensitive to sunlight, so inside the house they prefer deep carpet, bedding, and cracks and crevices.
- When you're done, throw the vacuum cleaner bag away—in an outside garbage can.
- Use a nontoxic flea-killing powder to treat your carpets (but remember, it does not control fleas elsewhere in the house). The powder stays deep in the carpet and kills fleas (using a form of boric acid) for up to a year.
- If you have a particularly serious flea problem, consider using a fogger or long-lasting spray to kill any adult and larval fleas, or having a professional exterminator treat your home.

skin can become infected, and antibiotics or more radical measures will be needed for a total cure.

Ticks can carry Lyme disease. Ticks will look like small round dots, about a sixteenth of an inch diameter, on your dog's skin. If you look with a magnifying glass, you'll see the tick's legs. When the tick attaches itself to the dog, it fills with blood and looks like a big grape hanging off the dog. Some topical flea treatments also include tick preventive, and you should consider using them if you live in a tick-infested area. In many areas of the country, veterinarians recommend a vaccination for Lyme disease.

Foxtails are sharp spikes that are found on grasses that have gone to seed. When they dry out in the spring and summer, they attach themselves to your

In your car:

- Take out the floor mats and hose them down with a strong stream of water, then hang them up to dry in the sun.
- Wash any towels, blankets, or other bedding you regularly keep in the car.
- Thoroughly vacuum the entire interior of your car, paying special attention to the seams between the bottom and back of the seats.
- When you're done, throw the vacuum cleaner bag away—in an outside garbage can.

In your yard:

- Flea larvae prefer shaded areas that have plenty of organic material and moisture, so rake the yard thoroughly and bag all the debris in tightly sealed bags.
- Spray your yard with an insecticide that has residual activity for at least thirty days. Insecticides that use a form of boric acid are nontoxic. Some products contain an insect growth regulator (such as fenoxycarb) and need to be applied only once or twice a year.
- For an especially difficult flea problem, consider having an exterminator treat your yard.
- Keep your yard free of piles of leaves, weeds, and other organic debris. Be especially careful in shady, moist areas, such as under bushes.

dog's fur and quickly embed in his skin, sometimes moving through the body into the bloodstream. They can cause an infection or abscess and can be particularly difficult to find and remove. After a hike, check your Basset's skin, especially between the toes and in the ears, for foxtails.

If all of this sounds time-consuming, be thankful you didn't select a breed that requires trimming and sculpting, like a Poodle! Most of what your Basset Hound needs to look and feel his best falls into the category of maintenance rather than beauty treatment. If you establish and follow a regular grooming routine, the end result will be a beautiful, healthy pet.

Chapter 8

Keeping Your Basset Hound Healthy

The Basset Hound generally is a hardy breed. But, like all dogs, she can be affected by genetic problems, illnesses, or injuries at some time in her life. By practicing preventive healthcare and keeping a watchful eye on your hound's condition and behavior, you'll be able to recognize problems early and help ensure your dog lives a long, healthy life.

Choosing a Veterinarian

Select a veterinarian before you even bring your puppy home. If you've had no previous relationship with a local veterinarian, ask your dog's breeder and other Basset owners in your area if they can recommend a vet with Basset Hound experience. Is the Basset Hound so unique that she needs a specialist? Not really, but it does help to have a vet who is aware of the problems that typically show up in your breed and also understands the Basset's physical idiosyncrasies.

Visit a few veterinarians and interview the staff. You will want to know if the clinic hours are convenient to your schedule. If there is more than one veterinarian, can you see the vet of your choice? Does the clinic provide twenty-four-hour service or does it use an emergency clinic for after-hours coverage? If the latter is the case, is the emergency clinic convenient for you?

At the same time, make sure you feel comfortable with the veterinarian's bedside manner. In addition to being considerate of your dog and her comfort, the vet should be willing to provide complete, nontechnical explanations of all diagnoses and procedures.

Your Puppy's First Vet Visit

Most breeders require that you have your new puppy examined within a few days to verify that the puppy was healthy when you brought her home. When you take the puppy for her first vet visit, bring along the inoculation and worming records the breeder gave you so your veterinarian can establish a comprehensive record and set up a schedule to complete the necessary vaccinations.

Health Concerns for Basset Hounds

For your own protection as well as your pet's, you should be familiar with the conditions to which Basset Hounds seem to be predisposed. These are health problems that also affect many other breeds. And, of course, not all Bassets have these problems. But some do. Your dog's breeder may have discussed some of these conditions with you.

Skeletal Problems

As a "dwarf" or chondrodystrophic breed with short legs, the Basset Hound is prone to some orthopedic ailments.

Herniated Disc

Back injury is a serious risk in all long-backed dogs. A herniated (ruptured) disc causes mild to severe symptoms, including weakness, pain, and even partial or full paralysis, depending on how severe the injury is and how many discs are ruptured. The rupture in the disc causes the inner nucleus of the disc to push out and pinch the spinal cord or nerves. Mild cases may be treated with steroids. More severe cases will require almost immediate surgery.

Have the veterinarian examine your puppy a few days after you bring her home.

   A dog with a herniated disc may walk with a wobbly gait and hunched up back. She may also appear to have pain in her neck and trouble lowering her head to eat.

Vaccines

What vaccines dogs need and how often they need them has been a subject of controversy for several years. Researchers, healthcare professionals, vaccine manufacturers, and dog owners do not always agree on which vaccines each dog needs or how often booster shots must be given.

In 2006, the American Animal Hospital Association issued a set of vaccination guidelines and recommendations intended to help dog owners and veterinarians sort through much of the controversy and conflicting information. The guidelines designate four vaccines as core, or essential for every dog, because of the serious nature of the diseases and their widespread distribution. These are canine distemper virus (using a modified live virus or recombinant modified live virus vaccine), canine parvovirus (using a modified live virus vaccine), canine adenovirus-2 (using a modified live virus vaccine), and rabies (using a killed virus). The general recommendations for their administration (except rabies, for which you must follow local laws) are:

- Vaccinate puppies at 6–8 weeks, 9–11 weeks, and 12–14 weeks.
- Give an initial "adult" vaccination when the dog is older than 16 weeks; two doses, three to four weeks apart, are

Prevention is the best cure. Don't allow your Basset to jump off furniture or down from the car. Help her up into the car, too. Avoid letting her use stairs as much as possible.

Hip Dysplasia

Hip dysplasia is a failure of the head of the femur (thighbone) to fit properly into the acetabulum (hip socket). A number of veterinarians have misdiagnosed hip dysplasia in Basset Hounds, failing to take into consideration the breed's unusual bone structure. Because of this structure, it would be virtually impossible advised, but one dose is considered protective and acceptable.

- Give a booster shot when the dog is 1 year old.
- Give a subsequent booster shot every three years, unless there are risk factors that make it necessary to vaccinate more or less often.

Noncore vaccines should only be considered for those dogs who risk exposure to a particular disease because of geographic area, lifestyle, frequency of travel, or other issues. They include vaccines against distemper-measles virus, canine parainfluenza virus, leptospirosis, Bordetella bronchiseptica, and *Borrelia burgdorferi* (Lyme disease).

Vaccines that are not generally recommended because the disease poses little risk to dogs or is easily treatable, or the vaccine has not been proven to be effective, are those against giardia, canine coronavirus, and canine adenovirus-1.

Often, combination injections are given to puppies, with one shot containing several core and noncore vaccines. Your veterinarian may be reluctant to use separate shots that do not include the noncore vaccines, because they must be specially ordered. If you are concerned about these noncore vaccines, talk to your vet.

for a Basset Hound to develop what would be considered "normal" hips in a breed with longer legs. The actual incidence of hip dysplasia in Basset Hounds is low, although some breeders have begun to have their dogs screened for this disorder through the Orthopedic Foundation for Animals (OFA).

Osteochondritis Dessicans

This condition of the shoulder is caused by cartilage trauma and results in severe lameness. It is usually seen in dogs between the ages of 6 months and 2 years. Extensive rest may help, but surgery may be necessary to repair the damage

This is the right way to lift a Basset Hound. You don't want to put any strain on her back.

caused by detached cartilage. Again, prevent your Basset Hound from jumping; this will protect the shoulder and forelegs from injury.

Panosteitis

Also called wandering lameness because it may switch from leg to leg, panosteitis is characterized by sudden onset of lameness due to an inflammation of the long bones of the legs. Pain and lameness usually appear first in the front legs, generally between the ages of 6 months and 2 years. Fever may accompany the lameness.

Because some veterinary manuals fail to list the Basset Hound as being among the breeds prone to panosteitis, you may need to inform your veterinarian that this, indeed, is a Basset Hound ailment. X-rays will diagnose panosteitis. The treatment is crate rest, time, and, if necessary, an analgesic for pain. Dogs will naturally grow out of this affliction.

Patella Luxation

In dogs with this condition, the patella, or kneecap, slips to one side as a result of defective grooves or ridges in the femur. This can be caused by an inherited defect or an injury. If the problem is hereditary, it generally will appear after the

How to Lift a Basset Hound

If you must lift your Basset Hound, an adult should do it, never a child, because the breed's long body is hard for a child to balance properly. The Basset's spinal column is prone to injury, and failure to support the back properly when lifting and carrying a Basset Hound can result in severe trauma.

To lift your dog, squat facing the dog's side. Place your forearms under the dog's body behind her front legs and in front of the hind legs, lifting both ends of the dog at the same time.

Better yet, get someone to help you lift the dog. Have the person holding the rear end cup one arm under the legs and hocks rather than letting the legs hang down.

If you are helping your Basset up onto the couch or into the car, place her front paws up, then hoist the back end up while supporting the dog's middle.

age of 6 months. An affected Basset will have a hitch in her gait, hiking up one rear leg as she runs. For serious cases, surgery can repair the problem.

Eye Problems

Basset Hounds may be prone to eye problems because of their prominent haw, or third eyelid—a membrane that is at the inner corner of the eye. Their drooping lower eyelid is more prominent than in other breeds and is therefore susceptible to injury and infection. Some eye problems in this breed can also be inherited.

Cherry Eye

Also known as gland prolapse, this condition is easily detected because a pink mass will show up in the inner corner of the eye. An infected tear gland on the surface of the third eyelid causes this condition. It usually occurs in puppies between the ages of 6 weeks and 1 year. Manual replacement of the gland may be attempted by your veterinarian, but surgery is usually necessary to replace the gland and secure it in position. If this fails, part of the gland may have to be removed.

Because of their drooping lower eyelids, Bassets are prone to eye injuries and infections.

Conjunctivitis

This inflammation of the third eyelid or the tissues lining the lids is caused by a collection of dirt, pollen, dust, and other foreign objects that tend to gather in the eyes of a dog whose nose is often to the ground. Eyewash can soothe the condition, but veterinary attention is needed.

Dry Eye

This condition sometimes develops in Basset Hounds because the sagging lower eyelid may droop more as a dog matures. Veterinary eyedrops will make her much more comfortable.

Glaucoma

This is the most serious of the eye ailments occurring in Basset Hounds. Symptoms include painful, bulging eyes and oversensitivity to light.

Glaucoma may be treated medically if the case is mild, and the dog's vision may be saved. In more severe cases, blindness will be the end result. The sightless Basset Hound's keen sense of smell compensates very efficiently for the eyesight loss. She can quickly learn to find her way around in familiar surroundings and live comfortably.

Other Basset Health Issues

Allergies

Dogs can be allergic to pollen, grass, grain in food, dust mites, or other allergens. Allergy signs include itching and dermatitis. It is often hard to determine what is causing the allergic reaction and testing by a veterinary dermatologist may be necessary. Treatment generally includes removing the allergen from the dog's environment and administering oral antihistamines.

> **TIP**
>
> Some breeders recommend an eye exam by a veterinary ophthalmologist for all Bassets by age 3 to screen for early stages of glaucoma and dry eye. Although expensive, these tests may save the dog's vision if treatment is started early.

Bloat

Bloat, or gastric dilation of the stomach, is a major risk in deep-chested breeds, including Basset Hounds. Prompt treatment is necessary if the animal is to survive. Bloat is often followed by torsion, in which the stomach twists.

Dogs can become allergic to all the same things we are allergic to, including grass and pollen. Canine allergies usually manifest as itchiness.

Symptoms are a hard, swollen abdomen, attempts to vomit, and obvious distress. A tube may be inserted into the stomach to relieve the gas if the stomach has not yet twisted. The dog also must be treated for shock. Once the stomach twists, surgery is required.

Dermatitis and Seborrhea

The Basset has a naturally oily coat, but extreme oiliness may mean something more serious. Symptoms of seborrhea and dermatitis include scaly skin (similar to dandruff); greasy, waxy, or crusty skin and hair; and odor. Shampoos and medication will relieve the symptoms, but overbathing can aggravate the condition. If not addressed, a secondary infection can develop. This is treated with antibiotics.

Hypothyroidism

Skin problems, lethargy, and weight gain can sometimes be attributed to insufficient production of the thyroid hormone. A simple blood test is used to diagnose this condition. It is easy to treat with daily medication throughout the dog's life.

Obesity

This was addressed in chapter 6, but it bears repeating. Obesity is a severe problem for long-backed breeds like Basset Hounds, because their spines and joints cannot carry excess weight without major stress. It can result in back and leg problems. Keep your dog at a healthy weight.

Thrombopathia and von Willebrand's Disease

These are hereditary bleeding disorders that interfere with blood clotting and could result in severe hemorrhage from a minor injury or during surgery. The severity can vary in individual Basset Hounds from minor bruising to uncontrollable bleeding. Tests can detect whether a dog suffers from either of these similar conditions. There is no cure, but the conditions can often be managed once your veterinarian is aware of them.

Common Canine Health Problems

Diarrhea

There are numerous reasons why dogs get diarrhea. Improper diet (including ingesting foreign objects), a food allergy, illness (either minor or serious),

Keep your dog at a good weight so she can stay active and healthy.

worms, and stress all may be contributing factors. In addition to pinpointing the cause, it is essential to prevent your dog from dehydrating during this period of distress. Since puppies dehydrate rather quickly, diarrhea in a youngster requires early veterinary intervention. In extreme cases, your dog may need to be hospitalized and put on intravenous fluids to overcome dehydration.

With an adult dog, have your veterinarian check a stool sample to determine if worms are present. Meanwhile, your veterinarian can dispense or recommend a good antidiarrheal medication. Dog food should be abandoned temporarily in favor of a bland diet of cooked rice combined with boiled hamburger or chicken. Assuming you are dealing with a minor upset and not a major illness, once the diarrhea clears up you should continue the bland diet for another forty-eight hours. Then *gradually* reintroduce dog food, a very small amount at a time.

Impacted Anal Glands

If your dog scoots along the floor and bites at her rear end, it could be a sign of impacted, or clogged, anal glands. (It might also indicate the presence of worms.) The anal sacs are located on the two lower sides of the anus and take on an oval shape when impacted. To empty them, cover the area with paper toweling and, starting from the bottom, push upwards toward the anal opening.

The liquid that squirts out has a nasty odor and should be gray or brown. If the liquid is bloody, consult your veterinarian. If this is more than you can

Why Spay and Neuter?

Breeding dogs is a serious undertaking that should only be part of a well-planned breeding program. Why? Because dogs pass on their physical and behavioral problems to their offspring. Even healthy, well-behaved dogs can pass on problems in their genes.

Is your dog so sweet that you'd like to have a litter of puppies just like her? If you breed her to another dog, the pups will not have the same genetic heritage she has. Breeding her *parents* again will increase the odds of a similar pup, but even then, the puppies in the second litter could inherit different genes. In fact, *there is no way to breed a dog to be just like another dog.*

Meanwhile, thousands and thousands of dogs are killed in animal shelters every year simply because they have no homes. Casual breeding is a big contributor to this problem.

If you don't plan to breed your dog, is it still a good idea to spay her or neuter him? Yes!

When you spay your female:

- You avoid her heat cycles, during which she discharges blood and scent.
- It greatly reduces the risk of mammary cancer and eliminates the risk of pyometra (an often fatal infection of the uterus) and uterine cancer.
- It prevents unwanted pregnancies.
- It reduces dominance behaviors and aggression.

When you neuter your male:

- It curbs the desire to roam and to fight with other males.
- It greatly reduces the risk of prostate cancer and eliminates the risk of testicular cancer.
- It helps reduce leg lifting and mounting behavior.
- It reduces dominance behaviors and aggression.

There is no way to breed a dog who is exactly like any other dog. Spay or neuter your pup.

handle, veterinarians and most groomers will do it for you. But do make sure it's not neglected, because the anal glands can become infected if the problem is not addressed.

Kennel Cough

Vaccines are available for many common strains of kennel cough. But, like the flu in humans, there are too many strains of this upper respiratory disease to make a vaccine effective against all of them. Kennel cough is highly contagious to other dogs and often spreads quickly through boarding kennels. Symptoms are coughing, runny nose, and sneezing. Your vet will most likely prescribe antibiotics and a cough suppressant, and recommend you keep your dog warm and comfortable.

Urinary Tract Infection

Symptoms of a urinary tract infection include excessive water consumption and frequent urination, often accompanied by straining and/or blood in the urine. Antibiotics will clear up the problem in two to three weeks. If your dog is suddenly having housetraining accidents, suspect urinary tract infection as one possible cause.

Vomiting

Like diarrhea, vomiting is usually the result of your Basset having eaten something she shouldn't. Call your veterinarian immediately if the vomitus is bloody or otherwise unusual; if your dog has other symptoms, including lethargy, lack of appetite, or fever; or if the vomiting persists.

Parasites

In addition to fleas and ticks, which have already been discussed in chapter 7, there are other parasites that can cause health problems for your Basset Hound.

Mites

Mites are tiny external parasites that can infest your dog in several different ways, each requiring a different type of treatment.

Ear Mites

Often the cause of ear infections in Basset Hounds, an affected dog will shake her head frequently and scratch at her ears. No larger than the head of a pin, your vet will be able to see ear mites under a microscope. Ear mites are highly

Mite infestations can be especially serious in young puppies.

contagious not only to other dogs but to cats as well, and will quickly spread to all the family's pets. Treatment consists of miticide eardrops, often combined with an antibiotic to combat infection.

Sarcoptic Mange

This mite causes extreme itching accompanied by hair loss, a rash, and oozing skin. Your vet will prescribe medications and possibly a miticide dip.

Demodectic Mange

More serious than sarcoptic mange, demodex is caused by mange mites that usually live on all dogs. Some seem to develop an autoimmune reaction. Medicated dips and antibiotics are indicated, but treatment must be started early if it is to be successful. Symptoms include hair loss around the eyes and on the face, usually in dogs under 1 year of age.

Intestinal Worms

Worms affect most dogs at some point. Your veterinarian can confirm the presence of worms by examining a stool sample under a microscope. Most worms are easily eliminated with medication. Prevent the spread of worms by cleaning up your dog's droppings daily and washing your hands immediately afterward.

Internal parasites are common in all puppies and most are routinely de-wormed.

Ascarids (Roundworms)

Puppies usually get roundworms from their mothers. They may pass them in their stool or, if severely infested, may vomit them up. Worms are common in puppies. Although roundworms, which look like moving spaghetti, do not present a serious threat to adult dogs, they can be fatal to young puppies if ignored.

Hookworms

A small and narrow parasite, hookworms often cause bloody diarrhea in the host dog. Veterinary intervention is required to keep your pet from becoming debilitated as a result of this parasite.

Tapeworms

Fleas transmit tapeworms to dogs. Segments of the worm's body, which resemble rice kernels, often break off and will be passed in the stool. They can often be seen stuck to the hair around a dog's anus.

Whipworms

These worms measure about two inches in length and can be very stubborn, usually requiring repeat treatments over a long period of time.

Parasite eggs can lurk in the soil and are easily ingested by dogs who always have their nose to the ground.

How to Make a Canine First-Aid Kit

If your dog hurts herself, even a minor cut, it can be very upsetting for both of you. Having a first-aid kit handy will help you to help her, calmly and efficiently. What should be in your canine first-aid kit?

- Antibiotic ointment
- Antiseptic and antibacterial cleansing wipes
- Benadryl
- Cotton-tipped applicators
- Disposable razor
- Elastic wrap bandages
- Extra leash and collar
- First-aid tape of various widths
- Gauze bandage roll
- Gauze pads of different sizes, including eye pads
- Hydrogen peroxide
- Instant cold compress
- Kaopectate or Pepto-Bismol tablets or liquid
- Latex gloves
- Lubricating jelly
- Muzzle
- Nail clippers
- Pen, pencil, and paper for notes and directions
- Plastic syringe with no needle (for administering liquids)
- Round-ended scissors and pointy scissors
- Safety pins
- Sterile saline eyewash
- Thermometer (rectal)
- Tweezers

Heartworms

Heartworms are transmitted by the bite of an infected mosquito. A severe infestation can be life-threatening. The adult worm lodges in the heart, where it reproduces and sends microfilariae (microscopic larvae) throughout the bloodstream. A dog may show no symptoms at all or may exhibit a dry cough, lethargy, weight loss, and ultimately suffer from lung problems and congestive heart failure.

Most veterinarians test dogs annually for the presence of heartworms. This is a quick, simple blood test, generally done before the onset of the mosquito season in your part of the country. Once a negative result is obtained, the dog can begin taking either daily or monthly heartworm preventive medicine.

If your Basset Hound tests positive, treatment is very hard on the dog. Complications are also common as the worms die and are eliminated from the bloodstream. Prevention, obviously, is the best choice. Many dog owners keep their pets on heartworm preventive year-round. The cost of the medication is a small price to pay considering the possible alternative. Heartworm and flea and tick preventives are often available combined into one monthly pill.

Giardia

This highly contagious parasite is actually a single-cell protozoa that enters your dog's system through infected water. If you go camping or hiking with your dog, the parasite can be easily ingested, so bring along clean drinking water for her as well as yourself.

Diarrhea, possibly with blood or mucus, is the principal sign of infection. Your vet will treat your Basset with oral medication. Thorough and frequent hand washing prevents giardia from spreading throughout the family's pets *and* people.

Because they are so heavy-bodied, Bassets do not fare well in hot weather. Protect yours when it's hot outside by taking her out in the cooler morning or evening.

Coccidia

Your Basset Hound can become infected with coccidia, another single-celled parasite, by eating infected soil or by licking her contaminated paws or fur. Symptoms include bloody, watery diarrhea and dehydration. It is also very contagious, especially among young puppies. Veterinarians treat coccidia with medication that helps your dog's immune system kill the parasites.

First Aid

It is important to know what constitutes an emergency and what ailments you can deal with safely at home. In some emergency situations, you will need to administer preliminary treatment before your dog arrives at the vet's office.

Curious, mouthy puppies will get into everything. Protect your pup by keeping your yard and home dog safe.

Bleeding

To control bleeding, apply direct pressure to the injury using a clean cloth or your hand. In Basset Hounds, the most common bleeding injury is to the ears. This also can be the most difficult area in which to control bleeding because of the dog's tendency to shake her head and restart the bleeding. Though torn ears rarely, if ever, are life-threatening, they can make your home or car look like a slaughterhouse and often will need stitches.

Heatstroke

Bassets are especially prone to heatstroke, and immediate action is necessary to avoid brain damage or death. Immerse the dog in cold water immediately. Once on-the-spot first

> **CAUTION**
>
> Never leave your Basset in the car on a warm day. Even in cool weather, the temperature inside a car gets very hot within ten to fifteen minutes and a dog will die from heatstroke.

ASPCA Animal Poison Control Center

The ASPCA Animal Poison Control Center has a staff of licensed veterinarians and board-certified toxicologists available 24 hours a day, 365 days a year. The number to call is (888) 426-4435. You will be charged a consultation fee of $60 per case, charged to most major credit cards. There is no charge for follow-up calls in critical cases. At your request, they will also contact your veterinarian. Specific treatment and information can be provided via fax.

Keep the poison control number in large, legible print with your other emergency telephone numbers. When you call, be prepared to give your name, address, and phone number; what your dog has gotten into (the amount and how long ago); your dog's breed, age, sex, and weight; and what signs and symptoms the dog is showing. You can log onto www.aspca.org and click on "Animal Poison Control Center" for more information, including a list of toxic and nontoxic plants.

aid has been provided, the dog should be wrapped in cold towels and rushed to the veterinarian.

Poisoning

Your dog's system will respond to different poisons in different ways. Common symptoms include vomiting, diarrhea, drooling, labored breathing, weakness, convulsions, or collapse. Try to determine the kind of poison your dog ingested so the poison control center operator or veterinarian will be able to provide the correct diagnosis and treatment.

Many common household substances are poisonous. Dogs like the sweet taste of antifreeze—one of the most dangerous toxins—which can cause kidney failure and death. There are now brands available without the ingredient etheneglycol that are a safer option.

Many houseplants can also be poisonous if ingested. Poisonous indoor plants include dieffenbachia, pothos, amaryllis, ivy, and umbrella plant. Toxic outdoor plants include oleander, foxglove, daffodil, azalea, mock orange, yew, periwinkle, morning glory, and larkspur.

Some garden products are extremely toxic to dogs. Cocoa mulch has the same dangerous ingredients as chocolate, which affect the nervous system, causing muscle tremors, seizures, and an irregular heartbeat. Snail bait, which unfortunately is especially attractive to dogs, can cause death within a few hours of ingestion. The major symptoms are twitching, drooling, and nervousness. Rodenticides (rat and mouse poison) contain strychnine, which can also quickly kill a pet.

Snakebites

If you live in an area where poisonous snakes are common, consider snake avoidance training for your Basset. Rattlesnake vaccines are available but do not provide complete protection in the case of a bite. If a poisonous snake bites your Basset Hound, quick administration of antivenin is vital to saving your pet's life. Try to identify the type of snake so you can tell the veterinarian.

Stings

A curious dog is likely to stick her nose in a bush full of bees and may even try to catch flying insects in her mouth. Keep an antihistamine (such as Benadryl)

All kinds of bees and bugs can sting or bite your dog. Make sure you know what to do if it happens.

When to Call the Veterinarian

Go to the vet right away or take your dog to an emergency veterinary clinic if:

- Your dog is choking
- Your dog is having trouble breathing
- Your dog has been injured and you cannot stop the bleeding within a few minutes
- Your dog has been stung or bitten by an insect and the site is swelling
- Your dog has been bitten by a snake
- Your dog has been bitten by another animal (including a dog) and shows any swelling or bleeding
- Your dog has touched, licked, or in any way been exposed to poison
- Your dog has been burned by either heat or caustic chemicals
- Your dog has been hit by a car
- Your dog has any obvious broken bones or cannot put any weight on one of her limbs
- Your dog has a seizure

Make an appointment to see the vet as soon as possible if:

- Your dog has been bitten by a cat, another dog, or a wild animal
- Your dog has been injured and is still limping an hour later

in your pet first-aid kit to give to a dog in distress from an insect sting. Symptoms include swelling, drooling, and difficulty breathing. The tweezers in your kit can be used to remove the stinger.

Trauma

An injured dog should be handled with extreme caution, both for your protection and hers. If possible, put on heavy-duty gloves before attempting to handle her. Even your own pet, if hurt and frightened, may bite under such circumstances. If you need to muzzle your Basset, wrap a long piece of cloth or a pair of pantyhose around her muzzle several times (leave her nose clear so she can breathe), and then bring the ends around the back of her head and tie them off.

Immediate veterinary care is necessary not only to treat possible injuries but for shock as well.

- Your dog has unexplained swelling or redness
- Your dog's appetite changes
- Your dog vomits repeatedly and can't seem to keep food down, or drools excessively while eating
- You see any changes in your dog's urination or defecation (pain during elimination, change in regular habits, blood in urine or stool, diarrhea, foul-smelling stool)
- Your dog scoots her rear end on the floor
- Your dog's energy level, attitude, or behavior changes for no apparent reason
- Your dog has crusty or cloudy eyes, or excessive tearing or discharge
- Your dog's nose is dry or chapped, hot, crusty, or runny
- Your dog's ears smell foul, have a dark discharge, or seem excessively waxy
- Your dog's gums are inflamed or bleeding, her teeth look brown, or her breath is foul
- Your dog's skin is red, flaky, itchy, or inflamed, or she keeps chewing at certain spots
- Your dog's coat is dull, dry, brittle, or bare in spots
- Your dog's paws are red, swollen, tender, cracked, or the nails are split or too long
- Your dog is panting excessively, wheezing, unable to catch her breath, breathing heavily, or sounds strange when she breathes

The Senior Citizen

Geriatric dogs need special care and rely on you to provide it. Most veterinarians will want to do a geriatric blood workup when your dog is about 8 years old to use as a baseline for evaluating her health during the senior years.

Physical Changes

Your older Basset's senses will not be as sharp as they were when she was an alert pup. She may not hear or see as well, and her reflexes may not be as sharp as they once were. She may become more sensitive to heat and cold, and less tolerant of rambunctious children, puppies, and changes in her routine. If you call her and she doesn't respond, stomp on the floor so the vibration will get her attention or tap on her shoulder; she probably just doesn't hear you.

Do everything you can to keep your old friend comfortable and happy.

Do everything you can to keep your older Basset comfortable. Keep a cozy bed for her away from drafts, and be patient with her slowness and stiff movement. There are many nice beds made especially for older dogs, including heated beds and those with memory-foam pads.

Exercise

Your Basset will walk more slowly as she ages, but it is still important to take her for a brief walk around the neighborhood. She needs the stimulation that seeing and smelling the world around her provides.

Senior Health Issues

Arthritis

Basset Hounds are particularly prone to this painful affliction because of their odd bone structure. Also, if your dog has suffered a back injury in the past, arthritis is more likely to develop as she gets older. An occasional buffered aspirin will help the average arthritic dog cope with the aches and pains, but in more extreme cases, and particularly when cold and/or wet weather prevails for an extended period, other measures may be needed. Ask your veterinarian.

Older dogs may stiffen up from arthritis. The Basset's bone structure makes this more likely.

Dental Care

A Basset's loose lips will gather and hold bacteria. Infection in the mouth can quickly spread throughout the body, which is why dental care is even more important for an older dog. Continue to brush your dog's teeth regularly and have the veterinarian check for excess tartar, broken teeth, and gum disease.

Eye Problems

Dry eye and glaucoma sometimes develop in elderly Basset Hounds, unrelated to hereditary causes. A veterinary ophthalmologist can diagnose and treat these conditions.

Tumors and Lumps

As your dog ages, she may develop an assortment of lumps and bumps. Some are just fatty tissue and can be left alone unless they enlarge or begin to leak fluid, while others may be cancerous and need to be removed. Your veterinarian can extract fluid from the lump and decide if surgery is needed.

Part III

Enjoying Your Basset Hound

Chapter 9

Training Your Basset Hound

by Peggy Moran

Training makes your best friend better! A properly trained dog has a happier life and a longer life expectancy. He is also more appreciated by the people he encounters each day, both at home and out and about.

A trained dog walks nicely and joins his family often, going places untrained dogs cannot go. He is never rude or unruly, and he always happily comes when called. When he meets people for the first time, he greets them by sitting and waiting to be petted, rather than jumping up. At home he doesn't compete with his human family, and alone he is not destructive or overly anxious. He isn't continually nagged with words like "no," since he has learned not to misbehave in the first place. He is never shamed, harshly punished, or treated unkindly, and he is a well-loved, involved member of the family.

Sounds good, doesn't it? If you are willing to invest some time, thought, and patience, the words above could soon be used to describe your dog (though perhaps changing "he" to "she"). Educating your pet in a positive way is fun and easy, and there is no better gift you can give your pet than the guarantee of improved understanding and a great relationship.

This chapter will explain how to offer kind leadership, reshape your pet's behavior in a positive and practical way, and even get a head start on simple obedience training.

Understanding Builds the Bond

Dog training is a learning adventure on both ends of the leash. Before attempting to teach their dog new behaviors or change unwanted ones, thoughtful dog owners take the time to understand why their pets behave the way they do, and how their own behavior can be either a positive or negative influence on their dog.

Canine Nature

Loving dogs as much as we do, it's easy to forget they are a completely different species. Despite sharing our homes and living as appreciated members of our families, dogs do not think or learn exactly the same way people do. Even if you love your dog like a child, you must remember to respect the fact that he is actually a dog.

Dogs have no idea when their behavior is inappropriate from a human perspective. They are not aware of the value of possessions they chew or of messes they make or the worry they sometimes seem to cause. While people tend to look at behavior as good and bad or right and wrong, dogs just discover what works and what doesn't work. Then they behave accordingly, learning from their own experiences and increasing or reducing behaviors to improve results for themselves.

You might wonder, "But don't dogs want to please us"? My answer is yes, provided your pleasure reflects back to them in positive ways they can feel and appreciate. Dogs do things for *dog* reasons, and everything they do works for them in some way or they wouldn't be doing it!

The Social Dog

Our pets descended from animals who lived in tightly knit, cooperative social groups. Though far removed in appearance and lifestyle from their ancestors, our dogs still relate in many of the same ways their wild relatives did. And in their relationships with one another, wild canids either lead or follow.

Canine ranking relationships are not about cruelty and power; they are about achievement and abilities. Competent dogs with high levels of drive and confidence step up, while deferring dogs step aside. But followers don't get the short end of the stick; they benefit from the security of having a more competent dog at the helm.

Our domestic dogs still measure themselves against other members of their group—us! Dog owners whose actions lead to positive results have willing, secure followers. But dogs may step up and fill the void or cut loose and do their own thing when their people fail to show capable leadership. When dogs are pushy, aggressive, and rude, or independent and unwilling, it's not because they have designs on the role of "master." It is more likely their owners failed to provide consistent leadership.

Dogs in training benefit from their handler's good leadership. Their education flows smoothly because they are impressed. Being in charge doesn't require you to physically dominate or punish your dog. You simply need to make some subtle changes in the way you relate to him every day.

Lead Your Pack!

Create schedules and structure daily activities. Dogs are creatures of habit and routines will create security. Feed meals at the same times each day and also try to schedule regular walks, training practices, and toilet outings. Your predictability will help your dog be patient.

Ask your dog to perform a task. Before releasing him to food or freedom, have him do something as simple as sit on command. Teach him that cooperation earns great results!

Give a release prompt (such as "let's go") when going through doors leading outside. This is a better idea than allowing your impatient pup to rush past you.

Pet your dog when he is calm, not when he is excited. Turn your touch into a tool that relaxes and settles.

Reward desirable rather than inappropriate behavior. Petting a jumping dog (who hasn't been invited up) reinforces jumping. Pet sitting dogs, and only invite lap dogs up after they've first "asked" by waiting for your invitation.

Replace personal punishment with positive reinforcement. Show a dog what *to do,* and motivate him to want to do it, and there will be no need to punish him for what he should *not do.* Dogs naturally follow, without the need for force or harshness.

Play creatively and appropriately. Your dog will learn the most about his social rank when he is playing with you. During play, dogs work to control toys and try to get the best of one another in a friendly way. The wrong sorts of play can create problems: For example, tug of war can lead to aggressiveness. Allowing your dog to control toys during play may result in possessive guarding when he has something he really values, such as a bone. Dogs who are chased during play may later run away from you when you approach to leash them. The right kinds of play will help increase your dog's social confidence while you gently assert your leadership.

How Dogs Learn (and How They Don't)

Dog training begins as a meeting of minds—yours and your dog's. Though the end goal may be to get your dog's body to behave in a specific way, training starts as a mind game. Your dog is learning all the time by observing the consequences of his actions and social interactions. He is always seeking out what he perceives as desirable and trying to avoid what he perceives as undesirable.

He will naturally repeat a behavior that either brings him more good stuff or makes bad stuff go away (these are both types of reinforcement). He will naturally avoid a behavior that brings him more bad stuff or makes the good stuff go away (these are both types of punishment).

Both reinforcement and punishment can be perceived as either the direct result of something the dog did himself, or as coming from an outside source.

Using Life's Rewards

Your best friend is smart and he is also cooperative. When the best things in life can only be had by working with you, your dog will view you as a facilitator. You unlock doors to all of the positively reinforcing experiences he values: his freedom, his friends at the park, food, affection, walks, and play. The trained dog accompanies you through those doors and waits to see what working with you will bring.

Rewarding your dog for good behavior is called positive reinforcement, and, as we've just seen, it increases the likelihood that he will repeat that behavior. The perfect reward is anything your dog wants that is safe and appropriate. Don't limit yourself to toys, treats, and things that come directly from you. Harness life's positives—barking at squirrels, chasing a falling leaf, bounding away from you at the dog park, pausing for a moment to sniff everything—and allow your dog to earn access to those things as rewards that come from cooperating with you. When he looks at you, when he sits, when he comes when you call—any prompted behavior can earn one of life's rewards. When he works with you, he earns the things he most appreciates; but when he tries to get those things on his own, he cannot. Rather than seeing you as someone who always says "no," your dog will view you as the one who says "let's go!" He will *want* to follow.

Purely Positive Reinforcement

With positive training, we emphasize teaching dogs what they should do to earn reinforcements, rather than punishing them for unwanted behaviors.

- Focus on teaching "do" rather than "don't." For example, a sitting dog isn't jumping.
- Use positive reinforcers that are valuable to your dog and the situation: A tired dog values rest; a confined dog values freedom.
- Play (appropriately)!
- Be a consistent leader.
- Set your dog up for success by anticipating and preventing problems.
- Notice and reward desirable behavior, and give him lots of attention when he is being good.
- Train ethically. Use humane methods and equipment that do not frighten or hurt your dog.
- When you are angry, walk away and plan a positive strategy.
- Keep practice sessions short and sweet. Five to ten minutes, three to five times a day is best.

What About Punishment?

Not only is it unnecessary to personally punish dogs, it is abusive. No matter how convinced you are that your dog "knows right from wrong," in reality he will associate personal punishment with the punisher. The resulting cowering, "guilty"-looking postures are actually displays of submission and fear. Later, when the punisher isn't around and the coast is clear, the same behavior he was punished for—such as raiding a trash can—might bring a self-delivered, very tasty result. The punished dog hasn't learned not to misbehave; he has learned to not get caught.

Does punishment ever have a place in dog training? Many people will heartily insist it does not. But dog owners often get frustrated as they try to stick to the path of all-positive reinforcement. It sure sounds great, but is it realistic, or even natural, to *never* say "no" to your dog?

A wild dog's life is not *all* positive. Hunger and thirst are both examples of negative reinforcement; the resulting discomfort motivates the wild dog to seek food and water. He encounters natural aversives such as pesky insects; mats in his coat; cold days; rainy days; sweltering hot days; and occasional run-ins with thorns, brambles, skunks, bees, and other nastiness. These all affect his behavior, as he tries to avoid the bad stuff whenever possible. The wild dog also occasionally encounters social punishers from others in his group when he gets too pushy. Starting with a growl or a snap from Mom, and later some mild and ritualized discipline from other members of his four-legged family, he learns to modify behaviors that elicit grouchy responses.

Our pet dogs don't naturally experience all positive results either, because they learn from their surroundings and from social experiences with other dogs. Watch a group of pet dogs playing together and you'll see a very old educational system still being used. As they wrestle and attempt to assert themselves, you'll notice many mouth-on-neck moments. Their playful biting is inhibited, with no intention to cause harm, but their message is clear: "Say uncle or this could hurt more!"

Observing that punishment does occur in nature, some people may feel compelled to try to be like the big wolf with their pet dogs. Becoming aggressive or heavy-handed with your pet will backfire! Your dog will not be impressed, nor will he want to follow you. Punishment causes dogs to change their behavior to avoid or escape discomfort and threats. Threatened dogs will either become very passive and offer submissive, appeasing postures, attempt to flee, or rise to the occasion and fight back. When people personally punish their dogs in an angry manner, one of these three defensive mechanisms will be triggered. Which one depends on a dog's genetic temperament as well as his past social experiences. Since we don't want to make our pets feel the need to avoid or escape us, personal punishment has no place in our training.

Remote Consequences

Sometimes, however, all-positive reinforcement is just not enough. That's because not all reinforcement comes from us. An inappropriate behavior can be self-reinforcing—just doing it makes the dog feel better in some way, whether you are there to say "good boy!" or not. Some examples are eating garbage, pulling the stuffing out of your sofa, barking at passersby, or urinating on the floor.

Although you don't want to personally punish your dog, the occasional deterrent may be called for to help derail these kinds of self-rewarding

The Problems with Personal Punishment

- Personally punished dogs are not taught appropriate behaviors.
- Personally punished dogs only stop misbehaving when they are caught or interrupted, but they don't learn not to misbehave when they are alone.
- Personally punished dogs become shy, fearful, and distrusting.
- Personally punished dogs may become defensively aggressive.
- Personally punished dogs become suppressed and inhibited.
- Personally punished dogs become stressed, triggering stress-reducing behaviors that their owners interpret as acts of spite, triggering even more punishment.
- Personally punished dogs have stressed owners.
- Personally punished dogs may begin to repeat behaviors they have been taught will result in negative, but predictable, attention.
- Personally punished dogs are more likely to be given away than are positively trained dogs.

misbehaviors. In these cases, mild forms of impersonal or remote punishment can be used as part of a correction. The goal isn't to make your dog feel bad or to "know he has done wrong," but to help redirect him to alternate behaviors that are more acceptable to you.

You do this by pairing a slightly startling, totally impersonal sound with an equally impersonal and *very mild* remote consequence. The impersonal sound might be a single shake of an empty plastic pop bottle with pennies in it, held out of your dog's sight. Or you could use a vocal expression such as "eh!" delivered with you looking *away* from your misbehaving dog.

Pair your chosen sound—the penny bottle or "eh!"—with either a slight tug on his collar or a sneaky spritz on the rump from a water bottle. Do this right *as* he touches something he should not; bad timing will confuse your dog and undermine your training success.

To keep things under your control and make sure you get the timing right, it's best to do this as a setup. "Accidentally" drop a shoe on the floor, and then help your dog learn some things are best avoided. As he sniffs the shoe say "eh!" without looking at him and give a *slight* tug against his collar. This sound will quickly become meaningful as a correction all by itself—sometimes after just one setup—making the tug correction obsolete. The tug lets your dog see that you were right; going for that shoe *was* a bad idea! Your wise dog will be more likely to heed your warning next time, and probably move closer to you where it's safe. Be a good friend and pick up the nasty shoe. He'll be relieved and you'll look heroic. Later, when he's home alone and encounters a stray shoe, he'll want to give it a wide berth.

Your negative marking sound will come in handy in the future, when your dog begins to venture down the wrong behavioral path. The goal is not to announce your disapproval or to threaten your dog. You are not telling him to stop or showing how *you* feel about his behavior. You are sounding a warning to a friend who's venturing off toward danger—"I wouldn't if I were you!" Suddenly, there is an abrupt, rather startling, noise! Now is the moment to redirect him and help him earn positive reinforcement. That interrupted behavior will become something he wants to avoid in the future, but he won't want to avoid you.

Practical Commands for Family Pets

Before you begin training your dog, let's look at some equipment you'll want to have on hand:

- **A buckle collar** is fine for most dogs. If your dog pulls *very* hard, try a head collar, a device similar to a horse halter that helps reduce pulling by turning the dog's head. *Do not* use a choke chain (sometimes called a training collar), because they cause physical harm even when used correctly.
- **Six-foot training leash and twenty-six–foot retractable leash.**
- **A few empty plastic soda bottles with about twenty pennies in each one.** This will be used to impersonally interrupt misbehaviors before redirecting dogs to more positive activities.

- **A favorite squeaky toy,** to motivate, attract attention, and reward your dog during training.

Baby Steps

Allow your young pup to drag a short, lightweight leash attached to a buckle collar for a few *supervised* moments, several times each day. At first the leash may annoy him and he may jump around a bit trying to get away from it. Distract him with your squeaky toy or a bit of his kibble and he'll quickly get used to his new "tail."

Lure your dog to take just a few steps with you on the leash by being inviting and enthusiastic. Make sure you reward him for his efforts.

Begin walking him on the leash by holding the end and following him. As he adapts, you can begin to assert gentle direct pressure to teach him to follow you. Don't jerk or yank, or he will become afraid to walk when the leash is on. If he becomes hesitant, squat down facing him and let him figure out that by moving toward you he is safe and secure. If he remains confused or frightened and does not come to you, go to him and help him understand that you provide safe harbor while he's on the leash. Then back away a few steps and try again to lure him to you. As he learns that you are the "home base," he'll want to follow when you walk a few steps, waiting for you to stop, squat down, and make him feel great.

So Attached to You!

The next step in training your dog—and this is a very important one—is to begin spending at least an hour or more each day with him on a four- to six-foot leash, held by or tethered to you. This training will increase his attachment to you—literally!—as you sit quietly or walk about, tending to your household business. When you are quiet, he'll learn it is time to settle; when you are active, he'll learn to move with you. Tethering also keeps him out of trouble when you are busy but still want his company. It is a great alternative to confining a dog, and can be used instead of crating any time you're home and need to slow him down a bit.

Rotating your dog from supervised freedom to tethered time to some quiet time in the crate or his gated area gives him a diverse and balanced day while he is learning. Two confined or tethered hours is the most you should require of your dog in one stretch, before changing to some supervised freedom, play, or a walk.

The dog in training may, at times, be stressed by all of the changes he is dealing with. Provide a stress outlet, such as a toy to chew on, when he is confined or tethered. He will settle into his quiet time more quickly and completely. Always be sure to provide several rounds of daily play and free time (in a fenced area or on your retractable leash) in addition to plenty of chewing materials.

Dog Talk

Tethering your dog is a great way to keep him calm and under control, but still with you.

Dogs don't speak in words, but they do have a language—body language. They use postures, vocalizations, movements, facial gestures, odors, and touch—usually with their mouths—to communicate what they are feeling and thinking.

We also "speak" using body language. We have quite an array of postures, movements, and facial gestures that accompany our touch and language as we attempt to communicate with our pets. And our dogs can quickly figure us out!

Alone, without associations, words are just noises. But, because we pair them with meaningful body language, our dogs make the connection. Dogs can really learn to understand much of what we *say*, if what we *do* at the same time is consistent.

The Positive Marker

Start your dog's education with one of the best tricks in dog training: Pair various positive reinforcers—food, a toy, touch—with a sound such as a click on a clicker (which you can get at the pet supply store) or a spoken word like "good!" or "yes!" This will enable you to later "mark" your dog's desirable behaviors.

It seems too easy: Just say "yes!" and give the dog his toy. (Or use whatever sound and reward you have chosen.) Later, when you make your marking sound right at the instant your dog does the right thing, he will know you are going to be giving him something good for that particular action. And he'll be eager to repeat the behavior to hear you mark it again!

Next, you must teach your dog to understand the meaning of cues you'll be using to ask him to perform specific behaviors. This is easy, too. Does he already do things you might like him to do on command? Of course! He lies down, he sits, he picks things up, he drops them again, he comes to you. All of the behaviors you'd like to control are already part of your dog's natural repertoire. The trick is getting him to offer those behaviors when you ask for them. And that means you have to teach him to associate a particular behavior on his part with a particular behavior on your part.

Sit Happens

Teach your dog an important new rule: From now on, he is only touched and petted when he is either sitting or lying down. You won't need to ask him to sit; in fact, you should not. Just keeping him tethered near you so there isn't much to do but stand, be ignored, or settle, and wait until sit happens.

He may pester you a bit, but be stoic and unresponsive. Starting now, when *you* are sitting down, a sitting dog is the only one you see and pay attention to. He will eventually sit, and as he does, attach the word "sit"—but don't be too excited or he'll jump right back up. Now mark with your positive sound that promises something good, then reward him with a slow, quiet, settling pet.

Training requires consistent reinforcement. Ask others to also wait until your dog is sitting and calm to touch him, and he will associate being petted with being relaxed. Be sure you train your dog to associate everyone's touch with quiet bonding.

Reinforcing "Sit" as a Command

Since your dog now understands one concept of working for a living—sit to earn petting—you can begin to shape and reinforce his desire to sit. Hold toys, treats, his bowl of food, and turn into a statue. But don't prompt him to sit! Instead, remain frozen and unavailable, looking somewhere out into space, over his head. He will put on a bit of a show, trying to get a response from you, and may offer various behaviors, but only one will push your button—sitting. Wait for him to offer the "right" behavior, and when he does, you unfreeze. Say "sit," then mark with an excited "good!" and give him the toy or treat with a release command—"OK!"

When you notice spontaneous sits occurring, be sure to take advantage of those free opportunities to make your command sequence meaningful and positive. Say "sit" as you observe sit happen—then mark with "good!" and praise, pet, or reward the dog. Soon, every time you look at your dog he'll be sitting and looking right back at you!

Now, after thirty days of purely positive practice, it's time to give him a test. When he is just walking around doing his own thing, suddenly ask him to sit. He'll probably do it right away. If he doesn't, do *not* repeat your command, or you'll just undermine its meaning ("sit" means sit *now;* the command is not "sit, sit, sit, sit"). Instead, get something he likes and let him know you have it. Wait for him to offer the sit—he will—then say "sit!" and complete your marking and rewarding sequence.

OK

"OK" will probably rate as one of your dog's favorite words. It's like the word "recess" to schoolchildren. It is the word used to release your dog from a command. You can introduce "OK" during your "sit" practice. When he gets up from a sit, say "OK" to tell him the sitting is finished. Soon that sound will mean "freedom."

Make it even more meaningful and positive. Whenever he spontaneously bounds away, say "OK!" Squeak a toy, and when he notices and shows interest, toss it for him.

Down

I've mentioned that you should only pet your dog when he is either sitting or lying down. Now, using the approach I've just introduced for "sit," teach your dog to lie down. You will be a statue, and hold something he would like to get but that you'll only release to a dog who is lying down. It helps to lower the desired item to the floor in front of him, still not speaking and not letting him have it until he offers you the new behavior you are seeking.

Lower your dog's reward to the floor to help him figure out what behavior will earn him his reward.

He may offer a sit and then wait expectantly, but you must make him keep searching for the new trick that triggers your generosity. Allow your dog to experiment and find the right answer, even if he has to search around for it first. When he lands on "down" and learns it is another behavior that works, he'll offer it more quickly the next time.

Don't say "down" until he lies down, to tightly associate your prompt with the correct behavior. To say "down, down, down" as he is sitting, looking at you, or pawing at the toy would make "down" mean those behaviors instead! Whichever behavior he offers, a training opportunity has been created. Once you've attached and shaped both sitting and lying down, you can ask for both behaviors with your verbal prompts, "sit" or "down." Be sure to only reinforce the "correct" reply!

Stay

"Stay" can easily be taught as an extension of what you've already been practicing. To teach "stay," you follow the entire sequence for reinforcing a "sit" or "down," except you wait a bit longer before you give the release word, "OK!" Wait a second or two longer during each practice before saying "OK!" and releasing your dog to the positive reinforcer (toy, treat, or one of life's other rewards).

You can step on the leash to help your dog understand the down-stay, but only do this when he is already lying down. You don't want to hurt him!

If he gets up before you've said "OK," you have two choices: pretend the release was your idea and quickly interject "OK!" as he breaks; or, if he is more experienced and practiced, mark the behavior with your correction sound— "eh!"— and then gently put him back on the spot, wait for him to lie down, and begin again. Be sure the next three practices are a success. Ask him to wait for just a second, and release him before he can be wrong. You need to keep your dog feeling like more of a success than a failure as you begin to test his training in increasingly more distracting and difficult situations.

As he gets the hang of it—he stays until you say "OK"— you can gradually push for longer times—up to a minute on a sit-stay, and up to three minutes on a down-stay. You can also gradually add distractions and work in new environments. To add a minor self-correction for the down-stay, stand on the dog's leash after he lies down, allowing about three inches of slack. If tries to get up before you've said "OK," he'll discover it doesn't work.

Do not step on the leash to make your dog lie down! This could badly hurt his neck, and will destroy his trust in you. Remember, we are teaching our dogs to make the best choices, not inflicting our answers upon them!

Come

Rather than thinking of "come" as an action—"come to me"—think of it as a place—"the dog is sitting in front of me, facing me." Since your dog by now really likes sitting to earn your touch and other positive reinforcement, he's likely to sometimes sit directly in front of you, facing you, all on his own. When this happens, give it a specific name: "come."

Now follow the rest of the training steps you have learned to make him like doing it and reinforce the behavior by practicing it any chance you get. Anything your dog wants and likes could be earned as a result of his first offering the sit-in-front known as "come."

You can help guide him into the right location. Use your hands as "landing gear" and pat the insides of your legs at his nose level. Do this while backing up a bit, to help him maneuver to the straight-in-front, facing-you position. Don't say the

Pat the insides of your legs to show your dog exactly where you like him to sit when you say "come."

word "come" while he's maneuvering, because he hasn't! You are trying to make "come" the end result, not the work in progress.

You can also help your dog by marking his movement in the right direction: Use your positive sound or word to promise he is getting warm. When he finally sits facing you, enthusiastically say "come," mark again with your positive word, and release him with an enthusiastic "OK!" Make it so worth his while, with lots of play and praise, that he can't wait for you to ask him to come again!

Building a Better Recall

Practice, practice, practice. Now, practice some more. Teach your dog that all good things in life hinge upon him first sitting in front of you in a behavior named "come." When you think he really has got it, test him by asking him to "come" as you gradually add distractions and change locations. Expect setbacks as you make these changes and practice accordingly. Lower your expectations and make his task easier so he is able to get it right. Use those distractions as rewards, when they are appropriate. For example, let him check out the interesting leaf that blew by as a reward for first coming to you and ignoring it.

Add distance and call your dog to come while he is on his retractable leash. If he refuses and sits looking at you blankly, *do not* jerk, tug, "pop," or reel him in. Do nothing! It is his move; wait to see what behavior he offers. He'll either begin to approach (mark the behavior with an excited "good!"), sit and do nothing (just keep waiting), or he'll try to move in some direction other than toward you. If he tries to leave, use your correction marker—"eh!"— and bring him to a stop by letting him walk to the end of the leash, *not* by jerking him. Now walk to him in a neutral manner, and don't jerk or show any disapproval. Gently bring him back to the spot where he was when you called him, then back away and face him, still waiting and not reissuing your command. Let him keep examining his options until he finds the one that works—yours!

If you have practiced everything I've suggested so far and given your dog a chance to really learn what "come" means, he is well aware of what you want and is quite intelligently weighing all his options. The only way he'll know your way is the one that works is to be allowed to examine his other choices and discover that they *don't* work.

Sooner or later every dog tests his training. Don't be offended or angry when your dog tests you. No matter how positive you've made it, he won't always want to do everything you ask, every time. When he explores the "what happens if I don't" scenario, your training is being strengthened. He will discover through his own process of trial and error that the best—and only—way out of a command he really doesn't feel compelled to obey is to obey it.

Let's Go

Many pet owners wonder if they can retain control while walking their dogs and still allow at least some running in front, sniffing, and playing. You might worry that allowing your dog occasional freedom could result in him expecting it all the time, leading to a testy, leash-straining walk. It's possible for both parties on the leash to have an enjoyable experience by implementing and reinforcing well-thought-out training techniques.

Begin by making word associations you'll use on your walks. Give the dog some slack on the leash, and as he starts to walk away from you say "OK" and begin to follow him.

Do not let him drag you; set the pace even when he is being given a turn at being the leader. Whenever he starts to pull, just come to a standstill and refuse to move (or refuse to allow him to continue forward) until there is slack in the leash. Do this correction without saying anything at all. When he isn't pulling, you may decide to just stand still and let him sniff about within the range the slack leash allows, or you may even mosey along following him. After a few minutes of "recess," it is time to work. Say something like "that's it" or "time's up," close the distance between you and your dog, and touch him.

Next say "let's go" (or whatever command you want to use to mean "follow me as we walk"). Turn and walk off, and, if he follows, mark his behavior with "good!" Then stop,

Give your dog slack on his leash as you walk and let him make the decision to walk with you.

When your dog catches up with you, make sure you let him know what a great dog he is!

Intersperse periods of attentive walking, where your dog is on a shorter leash, with periods on a slack leash, where he is allowed to look and sniff around.

squat down, and let him catch you. Make him glad he did! Start again, and do a few transitions as he gets the hang of your follow-the-leader game, speeding up, slowing down, and trying to make it fun. When you stop, he gets to catch up and receive some deserved positive reinforcement. Don't forget that's the reason he is following you, so be sure to make it worth his while!

Require him to remain attentive to you. Do not allow sniffing, playing, eliminating, or pulling during your time as leader on a walk. If he seems to get distracted—which, by the way, is the main reason dogs walk poorly with their people—change direction or pace without saying a word. Just help him realize "oops, I lost track of my human." Do not jerk his neck and say "heel"—this will make the word "heel" mean pain in the neck and will not encourage him to cooperate with you. Don't repeat "let's go," either. He needs to figure out that it is his job to keep track of and follow you if he wants to earn the positive benefits you provide.

The best reward you can give a dog for performing an attentive, controlled walk is a few minutes of walking without all of the controls. Of course, he must remain on a leash even during the "recess" parts of the walk, but allowing him to discriminate between attentive following—"let's go"—and having a few moments of relaxation—"OK"—will increase his willingness to work.

Training for Attention

Your dog pretty much has a one-track mind. Once he is focused on something, everything else is excluded. This can be great, for instance, when he's focusing on you! But it can also be dangerous if, for example, his attention is riveted on the bunny he is chasing and he does not hear you call—that is, not unless he has been trained to pay attention when you say his name.

When you call your dog's name, you will again be seeking a specific response—eye contact. The best way to teach this is to trigger his alerting response by making a noise with your mouth, such as whistling or a kissing sound, and then immediately doing something he'll find very intriguing.

You can play a treasure hunt game to help teach him to regard his name as a request for attention. As a bonus, you can reinforce the rest of his new vocabulary at the same time.

When you say your dog's name, you'll want him to make eye contact with you. Begin teaching this by making yourself so intriguing that he can't help but look.

Treasure Hunt

Make a kissing sound, then jump up and find a dog toy or dramatically raid the fridge and rather noisily eat a piece of cheese. After doing this twice, make a kissing sound and then look at your dog.

Of course he is looking at you! He is waiting to see if that sound—the kissing sound—means you're going to go hunting again. After all, you're so good at it! Because he is looking, say his name, mark with "good," then go hunting and find his toy. Release it to him with an "OK." At any point if he follows you, attach your "let's go!" command; if he leaves you, give permission with "OK."

Using this approach, he cannot be wrong—any behavior your dog offers can be named. You can add things like "take it" when he picks up a toy, and "thank you" when he happens to drop one. Many opportunities to make your new vocabulary meaningful and positive can be found within this simple training game.

Problems to watch out for when teaching the treasure hunt:

- You really do not want your dog to come to you when you call his name (later, when you try to engage his attention to ask him to stay, he'll already be on his way toward you). You just want him to look at you.
- Saying "watch me, watch me" doesn't teach your dog to *offer* his attention. It just makes you a background noise.

- Don't lure your dog's attention with the reward. Get his attention and then reward him for looking. Try holding a toy in one hand with your arm stretched out to your side. Wait until he looks at you rather than the toy. Now say his name then mark with "good!" and release the toy. As he goes for it, say "OK."

Teaching Cooperation

To get your dog's attention, try holding his toy with your arm out to your side. Wait until he looks at you, then mark the moment and give him the toy.

Never punish your dog for failing to obey you or try to punish him into compliance. Bribing, repeating yourself, and doing a behavior for him all avoid the real issue of dog training—his will. He must be helped to be willing, not made to achieve tasks. Good dog training helps your dog want to obey. He learns that he can gain what he values most through cooperation and compliance, and can't gain those things any other way.

Your dog is learning to *earn,* rather than expect, the good things in life. And you've become much more important to him than you were before. Because you are allowing him to experiment and learn, he doesn't have to be forced, manipulated, or bribed. When he wants something, he can gain it by cooperating with you. One of those "somethings"—and a great reward you shouldn't underestimate—is your positive attention, paid to him with love and sincere approval!

Chapter 10

Housetraining Your Basset Hound

Excerpted from Housetraining: An Owner's Guide to a Happy Healthy Pet, 1st Edition, *by September Morn*

By the time puppies are about 3 weeks old, they start to follow their mother around. When they are a few steps away from their clean sleeping area, the mama dog stops. The pups try to nurse but mom won't allow it. The pups mill around in frustration, then nature calls and they all urinate and defecate here, away from their bed. The mother dog returns to the nest, with her brood waddling behind her. Their first housetraining lesson has been a success.

The next one to housetrain puppies should be their breeder. The breeder watches as the puppies eliminate, then deftly removes the soiled papers and replaces them with clean papers before the pups can traipse back through their messes. He has wisely arranged the puppies' space so their bed, food, and drinking water are as far away from the elimination area as possible. This way, when the pups follow their mama, they will move away from their sleeping and eating area before eliminating. This habit will help the pups be easily housetrained.

Your Housetraining Shopping List

While your puppy's mother and breeder are getting her started on good house-training habits, you'll need to do some shopping. If you have all the essentials in place before your dog arrives, it will be easier to help her learn the rules from day one.

Newspaper: The younger your puppy and larger her breed, the more newspapers you'll need. Newspaper is absorbent, abundant, cheap, and convenient.

Puddle Pads: If you prefer not to stockpile newspaper, a commercial alternative is puddle pads. These thick paper pads can be purchased under several trade names at pet supply stores. The pads have waterproof backing, so puppy urine doesn't seep through onto the floor. Their disadvantages are that they will cost you more than newspapers and that they contain plastics that are not biodegradable.

Poop Removal Tool: There are several types of poop removal tools available. Some are designed with a separate pan and rake, and others have the handles hinged like scissors. Some scoops need two hands for operation, while others are designed for one-handed use. Try out the different brands at your pet supply store. Put a handful of pebbles or dog kibble on the floor and then pick them up with each type of scoop to determine which works best for you.

Plastic Bags: When you take your dog outside your yard, you *must* pick up after her. Dog waste is unsightly, smelly, and can harbor disease. In many cities and towns, the law mandates dog owners clean up pet waste deposited on public ground. Picking up after your dog using a plastic bag scoop is simple. Just put your hand inside the bag, like a mitten, and then grab the droppings. Turn the bag inside out, tie the top, and that's that.

Crate: To housetrain a puppy, you will need some way to confine her when you're unable to supervise. A dog crate is a secure way to confine your dog for short periods during the day and to use as a comfortable bed at night. Crates come in wire mesh and in plastic. The wire ones are foldable to store flat in a smaller space. The plastic ones are more cozy, draft-free, and quiet, and are approved for airline travel.

Baby Gates: Since you shouldn't crate a dog for more than an hour or two at a time during the day, baby gates are a good way to limit your dog's freedom in the house. Be sure the baby gates you use are safe. The old-fashioned wooden, expanding lattice type has seriously injured a number of children by collapsing and trapping a leg, arm, or neck. That type of gate can hurt a puppy, too, so use the modern grid-type gates instead. You'll need more than one baby gate if you have several doorways to close off.

Exercise Pen: Portable exercise pens are great when you have a young pup or a small dog. These metal or plastic pens are made of rectangular panels that are hinged together. The pens are freestanding, sturdy, foldable, and can be carried like a suitcase. You could set one up in your kitchen as the pup's daytime corral, and then take it outdoors to contain your pup while you garden or just sit and enjoy the day.

Enzymatic Cleaner: All dogs make housetraining mistakes. Accept this and be ready for it by buying an enzymatic cleaner made especially for pet accidents. Dogs like to eliminate where they have done it before, and lingering smells lead them to those spots. Ordinary household cleaners may remove all the odors you can smell, but only an enzymatic cleaner will remove everything your dog can smell.

The First Day

Housetraining is a matter of establishing good habits in your dog. That means you never want her to learn anything she will eventually have to unlearn. Start off housetraining on the right foot by teaching your dog that you prefer her to eliminate outside. Designate a potty area in your backyard (if you have one) or in the street in front of your home and take your dog to it as soon as you arrive home. Let her sniff a bit and, when she squats to go, give the action a name: "potty" or "do it" or anything else you won't be embarrassed to say in public. Eventually your dog will associate

Take your pup out frequently to her special potty spot and praise her when she goes.

Don't Overuse the Crate

A crate serves well as a dog's overnight bed, but you should not leave the dog in her crate for more than an hour or two during the day. Throughout the day, she needs to play and exercise. She is likely to want to drink some water and will undoubtedly eliminate. Confining your dog all day will give her no option but to soil her crate. This is not just unpleasant for you and the dog, but it reinforces bad cleanliness habits. And crating a pup for the whole day is abusive. Don't do it.

that word with the act and will eliminate on command. When she's finished, praise her with "good potty!"

That first day, take your puppy out to the potty area frequently. Although she may not eliminate every time, you are establishing a routine: You take her to her spot, ask her to eliminate, and praise her when she does.

Just before bedtime, take your dog to her potty area once more. Stand by and wait until she produces. Do not put your dog to bed for the night until she has eliminated. Be patient and calm. This is not the time to play with or excite your dog. If she's too excited, a pup not only won't eliminate, she probably won't want to sleep either.

Most dogs, even young ones, will not soil their beds if they can avoid it. For this reason, a sleeping crate can be a tremendous help during housetraining. Being crated at night can help a dog develop the muscles that control elimination. So after your dog has emptied out, put her to bed in her crate.

A good place to put your dog's sleeping crate is near your own bed. Dogs are pack animals, so they feel safer sleeping with others in a common area. In your bedroom, the pup will be near you and you'll be close enough to hear when she wakes during the night and needs to eliminate.

Pups under 4 months old often are not able to hold their urine all night. If your puppy has settled down to sleep but awakens and fusses a few hours later, she probably needs to go out. For the best housetraining progress, take your pup to her elimination area whenever she needs to go, even in the wee hours of the morning.

Your pup may soil in her crate if you ignore her late night urgency. It's unfair to let this happen, and it sends the wrong message about your expectations for

Very young puppies can't hold it in all night and may need an overnight trip outside.

cleanliness. Resign yourself to this midnight outing and just get up and take the pup out. Your pup will outgrow this need soon and will learn in the process that she can count on you, and you'll wake happily each morning to a clean dog.

The next morning, the very first order of business is to take your pup out to eliminate. Don't forget to take her to her special potty spot, ask her to eliminate, and then praise her when she does. After your pup empties out in the morning, give her breakfast, and then take her to her potty area again. After that, she shouldn't need to eliminate again right away, so you can allow her some free playtime. Keep an eye on the pup though, because when she pauses in play she may need to go potty. Take her to the right spot, give the command, and praise if she produces.

Confine Your Pup

A pup or dog who has not finished housetraining should *never* be allowed the run of the house unattended. A new dog (especially a puppy) with unlimited access to your house will make her own choices about where to eliminate. Vigilance during your new dog's first few weeks in your home will pay big dividends. Every potty mistake delays housetraining progress; every success speeds it along.

Prevent problems by setting up a controlled environment for your new pet. A good place for a puppy corral is often the kitchen. Kitchens almost always have waterproof or easily cleaned floors, which is a distinct asset with leaky pups. A bathroom, laundry room, or enclosed porch could be used for a puppy corral, but the kitchen is generally the best location. Kitchens are a meeting place and a hub of activity for many families, and a puppy will learn better manners when she is socialized thoroughly with family, friends, and nice strangers.

The way you structure your pup's corral area is very important. Her bed, food, and water should be at the opposite end of the corral from the potty area. When you first get your pup, spread newspaper over the rest of the floor of her playpen corral. Lay the papers at least four pages thick and be sure to overlap the edges. As you note the pup's progress, you can remove the papers nearest the sleeping and eating corner. Gradually decrease the size of the papered area until only the end where you want the pup to eliminate is covered. If you will be training your dog to eliminate outside, place newspaper at the end of the corral that is closest to the door that leads outdoors. That way as she moves away from the clean area to the papered area, the pup will also form the habit of heading toward the door to go out.

Maintain a scent marker for the pup's potty area by reserving a small soiled piece of paper when you clean up. Place this piece, with her scent of urine, under the top sheet of the clean papers you spread. This will cue your pup where to eliminate.

Most dog owners use a combination of indoor papers and outdoor elimination areas. When the pup is left by herself in the corral, she can potty on the ever-present newspaper. When you are available to take the pup outside, she can do her business in the outdoor spot. It is not difficult to switch a pup from indoor paper training to outdoor elimination. Owners of large pups often switch early, but potty papers are still useful if the pup spends time in her indoor corral while you're away. Use the papers as long as your pup needs them. If you come home and they haven't been soiled, you are ahead.

> **TIP**
>
> **Water**
>
> Make sure your dog has access to clean water at all times. Limiting the amount of water a dog drinks is not necessary for housetraining success and can be very dangerous. A dog needs water to digest food, to maintain a proper body temperature and proper blood volume, and to clean her system of toxins and wastes. A healthy dog will automatically drink the right amount. Do not restrict water intake. Controlling your dog's access to water is not the key to housetraining her; controlling her access to everything else in your home is.

Start your pup with a big area of paper to pee on; eventually, you can make it smaller.

When setting up your pup's outdoor yard, put the lounging area as far away as possible from the potty area, just as with the indoor corral setup. People with large yards, for example, might leave a patch unmowed at the edge of the lawn to serve as the dog's elimination area. Other dog owners teach the dog to relieve herself in a designated corner of a deck or patio. For an apartment-dwelling city dog, the outdoor potty area might be a tiny balcony or the curb. Each dog owner has somewhat different expectations for their dog. Teach your dog to eliminate in a spot that suits your environment and lifestyle.

Be sure to pick up droppings in your yard at least once a day. Dogs have a natural desire to stay far away from their own excrement, and if too many piles litter the ground, your dog won't want to walk through it and will start eliminating elsewhere. Leave just one small piece of feces in the potty area to remind your dog where the right spot is located.

To help a pup adapt to the change from indoors to outdoors, take one of her potty papers outside to the new elimination area. Let the pup stand on the paper when she goes potty outdoors. Each day for four days, reduce the size of the paper by half. By the fifth day, the pup, having used a smaller and smaller piece of paper to stand on, will probably just go to that spot and eliminate.

Take your pup to her outdoor potty place frequently throughout the day. A puppy can hold her urine for only about as many hours as her age in months, and will move her bowels as many times a day as she eats. So a 2-month-old pup

Take your dog out frequently for regularly scheduled walks.

will urinate about every two hours, while at 4 months she can manage about four hours between piddles. Pups vary somewhat in their rate of development, so this is not a hard and fast rule. It does, however, present a realistic idea of how long a pup can be left without access to a potty place. Past 4 months, her potty trips will be less frequent.

When you take the dog outdoors to her spot, keep her leashed so that she won't wander away. Stand quietly and let her sniff around in the designated area. If your pup starts to leave before she has eliminated, gently lead her back and remind her to go. If your pup sniffs at the spot, praise her calmly, say the command word, and just wait. If she produces, praise serenely, then give her time to sniff around a little more. She may not be finished, so give her time to go again before allowing her to play and explore her new home.

If you find yourself waiting more than five minutes for your dog to potty, take her back inside. Watch your pup carefully for twenty minutes, not giving her any opportunity to slip away to eliminate unnoticed. If you are too busy to watch the pup, put her in her crate. After twenty minutes, take her to the outdoor potty spot again and tell her what to do. If you're unsuccessful after five minutes, crate the dog again. Give her another chance to eliminate in fifteen or twenty minutes. Eventually, she will have to go.

Watch Your Pup

Be vigilant and don't let the pup make a mistake in the house. Each time you successfully anticipate elimination and take your pup to the potty spot, you'll move a step closer to your goal. Stay aware of your puppy's needs. If you ignore the pup, she will make mistakes and you'll be cleaning up more messes.

Keep a chart of your new dog's elimination behavior for the first three or four days. Jot down what times she eats, sleeps, and eliminates. After several days a pattern will emerge that can help you determine your pup's body rhythms. Most dogs tend to eliminate at fairly regular intervals. Once you know your new dog's natural rhythms, you'll be able to anticipate her needs and schedule appropriate potty outings.

Understanding the meanings of your dog's postures can also help you win the battle of the puddle. When your dog is getting ready to eliminate, she will display a specific set of postures. The sooner you can learn to read these signals, the cleaner your floor will stay.

A young puppy who feels the urge to eliminate may start to sniff the ground and walk in a circle. If the pup is very young, she may simply squat and go. All young puppies, male or female, squat to urinate. If you are housetraining a pup under 4 months of age, regardless of sex, watch for the beginnings of a squat as the signal to rush the pup to the potty area.

When a puppy is getting ready to defecate, she may run urgently back and forth or turn in a circle while sniffing or starting to squat. If defecation is imminent, the pup's anus may protrude or open slightly. When she starts to go, the pup will squat and hunch her back, her tail sticking straight out behind. There is no mistaking this posture; nothing else looks like this. If your pup takes this position, take her to her potty area. Hurry! You may have to carry her to get there in time.

A young puppy won't have much time between feeling the urge and actually eliminating, so you'll have to be quick to note her postural clues and intercept your pup in time. Pups from 3 to 6 months have a few seconds more between the urge and the act than younger ones do. The older your pup, the more time you'll have to get her to the potty area after she begins the posture signals that alert you to her need.

Accidents Happen

If you see your pup about to eliminate somewhere other than the designated area, interrupt her immediately. Say "wait, wait, wait!" or clap your hands loudly to startle her into stopping. Carry the pup, if she's still small enough, or take her collar and lead her to the correct area. Once your dog is in the potty area, give her the command to eliminate. Use a friendly voice for the command, then wait patiently for her to produce. The pup may be tense because you've just startled her and may have to relax a bit before she's able to eliminate. When she does her job, include the command word in the praise you give ("good potty").

The old-fashioned way of housetraining involved punishing a dog's mistakes even before she knew what she was supposed to do. Puppies were punished for breaking rules they didn't understand about functions they couldn't control. This was not fair. While your dog is new to housetraining, there is no need or excuse for punishing her mistakes. Your job is to take the dog to the potty area just before she needs to go, especially with pups under 3 months old. If you aren't watching your pup closely enough and she has an accident, don't punish the puppy for your failure to anticipate her needs. It's not the pup's fault; it's yours.

It's not fair to expect your baby puppy to be able to control herself the way an adult dog can.

In any case, punishment is not an effective tool for housetraining most dogs. Many will react to punishment by hiding puddles and feces where you won't find them right away (like behind the couch or under the desk). This eventually may lead to punishment after the fact, which leads to more hiding, and so on.

Instead of punishing for mistakes, stay a step ahead of potty accidents by learning to anticipate your pup's needs. Accompany your dog to the designated potty area when she needs to go. Tell her what you want her to do and praise her when she goes. This will work wonders. Punishment won't be necessary if you are a good teacher.

What happens if you come upon a mess after the fact? Some trainers say a dog can't remember having eliminated, even a few moments after she has done so. This is not true. The fact is that urine and feces carry a dog's unique scent, which she (and every other dog) can instantly recognize. So, if you happen upon a potty mistake after the fact, you can still use it to teach your dog.

But remember, no punishment! Spanking, hitting, shaking, or scaring a puppy for having a housetraining accident is confusing and counterproductive. Spend your energy instead on positive forms of teaching.

Take your pup and a paper towel to the mess. Point to the urine or feces and calmly tell your puppy, "no potty here." Then scoop or sop up the accident with the paper towel. Take the evidence and the pup to the approved potty area. Drop the mess on the ground and tell the dog, "good potty here," as if she had done the deed in the right place. If your pup sniffs at the evidence, praise her calmly. If the accident happened very recently, your dog may not have to go yet, but wait with her a few minutes anyway. If she eliminates, praise her. Afterwards, go finish cleaning up the mess.

Soon the puppy will understand that there is a place where you are pleased about elimination and other places where you are not. Praising for elimination in the approved place will help your pup remember the rules.

Scheduling Basics

With a new puppy in the home, don't be surprised if your rising time is suddenly a little earlier than you've been accustomed to. Puppies have earned a reputation as very early risers. When your pup wakes you at the crack of dawn, you will have to get up and take her to her elimination spot. Be patient. When your dog is an adult, she may enjoy sleeping in as much as you do.

At the end of the chapter, you'll find a typical housetraining schedule for puppies aged 10 weeks to 6 months. (To find schedules for younger and older pups, and for adult dogs, visit this book's companion web site.) It's fine to adjust the rising times when using this schedule, but you should not adjust the intervals between feedings and potty outings unless your pup's behavior justifies a change. Your puppy can only meet your expectations in housetraining if you help her learn the rules.

The schedule for puppies is devised with the assumption that someone will be home most of the time with the pup. That would be the best scenario, of course, but is not always possible. You may be able to ease the problems of a latchkey pup by having a neighbor or friend look in on the pup at noon and take her to eliminate. A better solution might be hiring a pet sitter to drop by midday. A professional pet sitter will be knowledgeable about companion

Housetraining is a huge task, but it doesn't go on forever. Be patient and soon your dog will be reliable.

animals and can give your pup high-quality care and socialization. Some can even help train your pup in both potty manners and basic obedience. Ask your veterinarian and your dog-owning friends to recommend a good pet sitter.

If you must leave your pup alone during her early housetraining period, be sure to cover the entire floor of her corral with thick layers of overlapping newspaper. If you come home to messes in the puppy corral, just clean them up. Be patient—she's still a baby.

Use this schedule (and the ones on the companion web site) as a basic plan to help prevent housetraining accidents. Meanwhile, use your own powers of observation to discover how to best modify the basic schedule to fit your dog's unique needs. Each dog is an individual and will have her own rhythms, and each dog is reliable at a different age.

Schedule for Pups 10 Weeks to 6 Months

7:00 a.m.	Get up and take the puppy from her sleeping crate to her potty spot.
7:15	Clean up last night's messes, if any.
7:30	Food and fresh water.
7:45	Pick up the food bowl. Take the pup to her potty spot; wait and praise.
8:00	The pup plays around your feet while you have your breakfast.
9:00	Potty break (younger pups may not be able to wait this long).
9:15	Play and obedience practice.
10:00	Potty break.

10:15	The puppy is in her corral with safe toys to chew and play with.
11:30	Potty break (younger pups may not be able to wait this long).
11:45	Food and fresh water.
12:00 p.m.	Pick up the food bowl and take the pup to her potty spot.
12:15	The puppy is in her corral with safe toys to chew and play with.
1:00	Potty break (younger pups may not be able to wait this long).
1:15	Put the pup on a leash and take her around the house with you.
3:30	Potty break (younger pups may not be able to wait this long).
3:45	Put the pup in her corral with safe toys and chews for solitary play and/or a nap.
4:45	Potty break.
5:00	Food and fresh water.
5:15	Potty break.
5:30	The pup may play nearby (either leashed or in her corral) while you prepare your evening meal.
7:00	Potty break.
7:15	Leashed or closely watched, the pup may play and socialize with family and visitors.
9:15	Potty break (younger pups may not be able to wait this long).
10:45	Last chance to potty.
11:00	Put the pup to bed in her crate for the night.

Learning More About Your Basset Hound

Books

About Basset Hounds

Booth, Robert E., *The Official Book of the Basset Hound*, TFH Publications, 1999.

Morgan, Diane, *The Basset Hound Owner's Survival Guide*, Howell Book House, 1998.

Smith, Carl E., *Basset Hounds and Beagles—With Descriptive and Historical Sketches on Each Breed, Their Breeding, and Use as a Sporting Dog*, Vintage Dog Books, 2006.

Dog Training

Kilcommons, Brian, and Sarah Wilson, *Good Owners, Great Dogs*, Grand Central Publishing, 1999.

The Monks of New Skete, *The Art of Raising a Puppy*, Little, Brown and Co., 2002.

Palika, Liz, *All Dogs Need Some Training*, Howell Book House, 1997.

Pelar, Colleen, CPDT, *Living with Kids & Dogs . . . Without Losing Your Mind*, C&R Publishing, 2005.

Volhard, Jack, and Wendy Volhard, *Dog Training For Dummies*, 2nd Edition, John Wiley & Sons, 2005.

Dog Sports and Activities

Coile, D. Caroline, PhD, *Beyond Fetch: Fun, Interactive Activities for You and Your Dog*, Howell Book House, 2003.

Davis, Kathy Diamond, *Therapy Dogs: Training Your Dog to Reach Others*, Dogwise Publishing, 2002.

John, A. Meredith, and Carole L. Richards, *Raising a Champion: A Beginner's Guide to Showing Dogs*, The Well Trained Dog, 2001.

Sanders, William, *Enthusiastic Tracking: The Step-by-Step Training Manual*, Rime Publications, 1998.

Simmons-Moake, Jane, *Agility Training: The Fun Sport for All Dogs*, Howell Book House, 1992.

Healthcare and Nutrition

Borzendowski, Janice, *Caring for Your Aging Dog*, Sterling, 2006.

Eldredge, Debra M. DVM, Liisa D. Carlson, DVM, Delbert G. Carlson, DVM, James Giffin, MD, *Dog Owner's Home Veterinary Handbook*, 4th Edition, Howell Book House, 2007.

Palika, Liz, *The Ultimate Dog Treat Cookbook: Homemade Goodies for Man's Best Friend*, Howell Book House, 2005.

Volhard, Wendy, and Kerry Brown, DVM, *Holistic Guide for a Healthy Dog*, 2nd Edition, Howell Book House, 2000.

Fiction Featuring Basset Hounds

Handler, David, *The Man Who Died Laughing*, Busted Flush Press, 2006.

A series of murder mysteries featuring Stewart "Hoagy" Hoag, an amateur private eye, and his Basset Hound, Lulu.

Olsen, Mary-Kate and Ashley, *The Case of the Cheerleading Camp Mystery*, Harper Entertainment, 2000.

One of the New Adventures of Mary-Kate and Ashley, *a series of books featuring the Trenchcoat Twins and their Basset Hound, Clue.*

Magazines

AKC Gazette
AKC Family Dog
American Kennel Club
260 Madison Ave.
New York, NY 10016
www.akc.org

The Bugler
5972 Francis Ferry Rd.
McMinnville, TN 37110
www.bugler-bassethoundmagazine.com

Dog Fancy
Bow Tie, Inc.
P.O. Box 6050
Mission Viejo, CA 92690
www.dogfancy.com

Dogs for Kids
Bow Tie, Inc.
P.O. Box 6050
Mission Viejo, CA 92690
www.dogsforkids.com

Dog World
Bow Tie, Inc.
P.O. Box 6050
Mission Viejo, CA 92690
www.dogworldmag.com

Clubs, Registries, and Associations

Basset Hound Club of America
www.basset-bhca.org
This is the national club for the breed; its web site has a great deal of information, including upcoming shows and competitions. There are also many all-breed, individual breed, canine sport, and other special-interest dog clubs across the country. The registries listed below can help you find clubs in your area.

American Kennel Club
260 Madison Ave.
New York, NY 10016
(212) 696-8200
www.akc.org

Canadian Kennel Club
200 Ronson Dr.
Etobicoke, Ontario
Canada M9W 5Z9
(800) 250-8040 or (416) 675-5511
www.ckc.ca

United Kennel Club
100 E. Kilgore Rd.
Kalamazoo, MI 49002
(616) 343-9020
www.ukcdogs.com

Delta Society
875 124th Ave. NE, Suite 101
Bellevue, WA 98005-2531
(425) 679-5500
www.deltasociety.org

Therapy Dogs International
88 Bartley Rd.
Flanders, New Jersey 07836
(973) 252-9800
www.tdi-dog.org

United States Dog Agility Association
P.O. Box 850955
Richardson, TX 75085
(972) 487-2200
www.usdaa.com

Internet Resources

Basset Hounds

The Daily Drool
www.dailydrool.com
Fun site for Basset Hound lovers to learn and share Basset Hound stories, photos, and information. Discussion groups, songs, and shopping are just a few of the many features.

CyberHound: The Basset Hound Homepage
www.basset.net
Education, information, and lots of links to Basset Hound resources. Includes an open forum where you can browse discussions about healthcare, performance events, rescue, and other topics.

Families and Dogs

Living with Kids and Dogs
www.livingwithkidsanddogs.com
Colleen Pelar, CPDT, CDBC, maintains this site for families with children and dogs. Lots of safety information and kid-friendly activities.

Doggone Safe
www.doggonesafe.com
Nonprofit site dedicated to dog-bite prevention.

How to Love Your Dog
www.loveyourdog.com
A children's guide to dogs. Includes tricks, training, games, and care tips.

Canine Health

American Animal Hospital Association

www.healthypet.com

You'll find an extensive pet care library from the American Animal Hospital Association.

PetDoc

www.petdoc.com

Library of health, behavior, and care articles, searchable by symptom and subject.

The Pet Center

www.thepetcenter.com

Written and photographed by veterinarians in actual animal hospital settings, this site presents pet healthcare information in an easily understood way.

Dog Sports and Activities

Dog Patch

www.dogpatch.org

Information on many different dog sports and activities. There's also a gateway to links on almost every dog subject you can think of.

Dog Play

www.dog-play.com

More about dog sports and activities, including hiking, backpacking, therapy dog work, and lots of items for kids.

Other Resources

Pet Connection

www.petconnection.com

All about pets, including product reviews, blogs, questions and answers, and more. Written by dog experts and veterinarians.

Dog Friendly

www.dogfriendly.com

Links to dog friendly parks, travel, attractions, apartments, beaches, and everything doggie.

Index

adoption, 33–35
adult dog, 32, 58–60
allergies, 85
American Kennel Club (AKC), 19, 21, 36
anal gland impaction, 87, 89
arthritis, 100
ascarids (roundworms), 92
ASPCA Animal Poison Control Center, 96
athletic ability, 15
attention, training, 120–122

baby gates, 124–125
BARF (bones and raw food) diet, 61
Basset Hound Club
   of America, 12, 19, 21, 36
bathing, 69–72
biting, 53–54
bleeding, controlling, 95
bloat, 59–60, 85–86
body, breed standard for, 14
body language, 113
bones, 62
breeder
      housetraining by, 123
      kennel name, 50
      obtaining puppy from, 35–39
      questions from, 38–39
breed standard, 12–16
bring your puppy home, 50–51

characteristics of breed, 23–26
cherry eye, 83
chew toys, 43
children, 23, 52–54
chocolate, toxicity of, 67
choke chain, 111
choosing your Basset Hound
      adoption, 33–35
      age, 32

      gender, 31
      multiple dogs, 33
      pet-quality or show-quality, 33
      where to get a puppy, 35–38
cleanup supplies, 124, 125
clicker, training use of, 113
coat, 15
coccidia, 95
collar, 43, 48, 111
color, 15
commands
      come, 117–118
      down, 115–116
      for elimination, 125, 127, 132
      let's go, 119–120
      OK, 115
      sit, 114–115
      stay, 116–117
conjunctivitis, 84
cooperation, teaching, 122
corral, puppy, 128
crate
      for housetraining, 126–127
      location, 44
      overuse of, 126
      selecting, 43, 45, 124
      uses for, 42–44

demodectic mange, 91
dental care, 74–75, 101
dermatitis, 86
dewlap, 14
diarrhea, 86–87
dishes, food and water, 43
drool, 25
dry eye, 84, 101

ear mites, 90–91
ears
    breed standard, 14
    cleaning, 74
emergencies, 95–99
enzymatic cleaner, 125
exercise pen, 45, 125
eye contact, 120
eyes
    breed standard, 14
    examination, 85
    health problems, 83–84, 101

female dog, choosing, 31
first aid, 95–99
first-aid kit, 93
fleas
    checking for, 75
    controlling in environment, 76–77
    preventives for controlling, 70
food
    adult dog, 58–60
    bland for diarrhea, 87
    bloat risk and, 59–60
    canned, 62
    dry (kibble), 61
    free feeding, 58
    labels, 64
    overweight dogs, 64–65
    people, 66
    picky eaters, 66–67
    poisonous, 67
    puppy, 57–58
    raw and homemade, 61–62
    semimoist, 62–63
    senior dog, 60
    snacks and treats, 63
    switching, 61
    vitamins and supplements, 63
foxtails, 76–77

giardia, 94
glaucoma, 84, 101
grooming
    bathing, 69–72
    ears cleaning, 74
    nail trimming, 73
    skin care, 75–77
    supplies, 68–69

teeth cleaning, 74–75
tools, 43

head, breed standard for, 14
health issues. See also specific disorders
    in poorly bred dogs, 37–38
    in senior dogs, 99–100
heartworms, 93–94
heatstroke, 95–96
hereditary defects, 38
herniated disc, 79–80
hip dysplasia, 80–81
history, of breed, 17–22
home
    flea control, 76–77
    puppy-proofing, 46–47
hookworms, 92
housetraining
    accidents, 132–133
    anticipating need to eliminate, 131
    by breeder, 123
    charting elimination behavior, 131
    cleanup, 124, 125, 129, 133
    crate use, 126–127
    elimination area, 125–131
    first day, 125–127
    indoor to outdoor switching
        techniques, 128–130
    by mother dog, 123
    newspaper use, 124, 128–129
    pet sitter, 134
    punishment, 132–133
    puppy corral use, 128
    scent marker, 128
    schedule, 133–135
    shopping list, 124–125
    water access, 128
hunting, 11, 12, 18, 19, 26
hypothyroidism, 86

identification, 48–49
independence, of breed, 16
insect growth regulators (IGRs), 70
instincts, 25–26

jumping, 28, 53–54

kennel cough, 89
kindergarten, puppy, 54–56

leadership, 105–106
leash
    choosing, 43
    for training, 111, 112
legs, breed standard for, 14
license, 49
lifting your dog, 82, 83
limited registration, 33
lumps, 101

male dog, choosing, 31
mange, 91
marker, positive, 113–114
microchip, 48–49
mites, 90–91

nail cutters, 43
nail trimming, 73
name, choosing, 49–50
neutering, 88
newspaper, housetraining use, 124,
    128–129

obedience trials, 30
obesity, 64–65, 86
origin, of breed, 17–18
Orthopedic Foundation for Animals (OFA),
    81
osteochondritis dessicans, 81–82
overweight dogs, 64–65
owners, famous, 20

panosteitis, 82
parasites, 90–95
patella luxation, 82–83
pet sitter, 52, 134
plants, toxic, 96–97
play, training during, 106–107
play-biting, 53–54
poisoning, 67, 96–97
poop removal tools, 124
popular culture, Basset Hounds in, 20–22
positive reinforcement, 106, 107, 108
puddle pads, housetraining use, 124
punishment, 106, 108–109, 110, 132–133
puppy
    evaluating litter, 36–37
    feeding, 57–58
    first few weeks with, 50–52

housetraining, 123–135
pet-quality or show-quality, 33
schedule for, 52
supplies for, 43
training and socialization, 54–56
vaccination, 80–81
puppy-proofing your home, 46–47

recall, training techniques, 118
registration, 33, 50
release word/prompt, 106, 114, 115,
    116–117, 121
remote consequences, 109–111
rescue groups, 32, 33–35
reward, training, 106, 107, 108
roundworms, 92

sarcoptic mange, 91
scenthound, 11–12, 25
scent marker, 128
schedule
    housetraining, 133–135
    puppy, 52
seborrhea, 86
senior dog
    choosing, 35
    exercise, 100
    feeding, 60
    health issues, 100–101
    physical changes, 99–100
senses, 27
separation anxiety, 51
shampoo, 69, 71
shelters, obtaining dog from, 33–35
size, breed standard for, 13–14
skeletal problems, 79–83
skin care, 75–77
snacks, 63
snake bites, 97
socialization, 54–56
social rank, 105–106
spaying, 88
sports, 30
stings, 97–98
supplements, 63

tag, ID, 48
tail, breed standard for, 14
tapeworms, 92

teeth cleaning, 74–75
temperament, 16, 28–29
tethering, training technique, 112–113
thrombopathia, 38, 86
ticking, 15
tick removal, 72, 76
toothpaste, 75
toys, 43, 48, 106, 112
trainer, 55
training
        attention, 120–122
        beginning, 54–56
        benefits of, 104
        breed characteristics, 28–29
        canine nature, 105
        come command, 117–118
        cooperation, 122
        down command, 115–116
        equipment, 111–112
        how dogs learn, 107
        leadership, 105–106
        leash introduction, 112
        let's go command, 119–120
        life's rewards, 107
        OK command, 115
        during play, 106–107
        positive marker, 113–114
        positive reinforcement, 106, 107, 108
        punishment, 106, 108–109, 110
        recall command, 118
        remote consequences, 109–111

sit command, 114–115
stay command, 116–117
        tethering, 112–113
trauma, 98
treasure hunt, training game, 120–121
treats, 63
tug of war, aggressiveness from, 106
tumors, 101

urinary tract infection, 89

vaccines, 80–81
veterinarian
        choosing, 78
        first visit to, 79
        when to call, 98–99
vitamins, 63
vocalization, 16
vomiting, 90
von Willebrand's disease, 38, 86

water, 60, 128
weight
        breed standard for, 13
        overweight dogs, 64–65, 86
whipworms, 92
worms, intestinal, 91–92

yard
        flea control, 77
        puppy-proofing, 47

Photo Credits:

Isabelle Francais: 1, 14, 20, 22, 29, 31, 32, 39, 40–41, 42, 44, 51, 52, 53, 56,
    57, 58, 67, 71, 74, 78, 79, 89, 90, 91, 94, 95, 101, 123, 125, 127, 129, 132
Melanie Snowhite: 4–5, 11, 15, 16, 17, 24, 34, 68, 69, 82, 102–103, 104
Tammy Raabe Rao/rubicat: 8–9, 84
jeanmfogle.com: 12, 19, 23, 25, 28, 30, 45, 48, 49, 59, 61, 63, 65, 73, 75, 87,
    92, 97, 100, 134
Bonnie Nance: 35, 37
Terry Albert: 62, 85, 130